W9-CSH-610

SAN JOAQUIN VALLEY LIBRARY SYSTEM
1019252467

Egg Craft

Dedicated to eggers everywhere—
past, present, and future

Egg Craft

Written and illustrated by
Arden J. Newsome

Lothrop, Lee & Shepard Company / *New York*

Also by Arden J. Newsome

MAKE IT WITH FELT:
An Art & Craft Book

SPOOLCRAFT

Library of Congress Cataloging in Publication Data

Newsome, Arden J.
Egg craft.

SUMMARY: Demonstrates in text and illustrations the various techniques of decorating blown or cooked eggs. Includes a list of suppliers of materials used.
Bibliography: p. 124
1. Egg decoration—Juvenile literature. [1. Egg decoration. 2. Handicraft] I. Title.
TT896.7.N48 745.59′4 72-11993
ISBN 0-688-41512-1
ISBN 0-688-45512-3 (lib. bdg.)

2 3 4 5 77 76 75 74 73

Contents

How to Be an Egger

No doubt you look forward each year to decorating eggs at Easter. Nearly everyone has enjoyed this holiday experience. But do you know that egg decorating need not be a once-a-year occurrence?

Thousands of people—men, women, and children—consider egg-crafting, or egging, a very serious full-time hobby. These people who create with eggs are called "eggers." Eggers decorate and work with eggs all year round. And they do everything from painting them with colorful and intricate designs to cutting doors, windows, and openings in the shell with scissors or special tools.

To an egger, the most desirable part of any egg is the part that most people throw away. The shells of chicken, turkey, duck, goose, and even ostrich eggs are the basic ingredient of their joyous craft. With these shells, beaded, hand-painted, découpage, jeweled, and beribboned eggs are created. Satin-lined and hinged jewel boxes, miniature replicas of "Gone With the Wind" lamps, flower baskets, and birdcages are developed.

There are even jeweled eggs with hinged doors that open to reveal a miniature scene, a revolving ballerina, a watch, or a tiny Nativity. The variety and number of eggs an egger creates are unbelievable. There are eggs for every holiday including Easter and Christmas, eggs for every occasion such as weddings, birth, and graduation, and eggs for no rhyme or reason like Cinderella coaches, sailing ships, ascension balloons, tea sets, and Christmas tree lights.

Egg decorating began long ago in the days of ancient Egypt, Greece, and Rome, when eggs were the symbol of spring and represented the rebirth of life. At that time eggs were very scarce, so they were usually colored in some way and given as gifts—not to be eaten but to be kept and treasured for years and years.

As eggs became more plentiful, the art of decorating and coloring them became widespread among most of the peoples of the world. The colors and designs used were usually symbolic of different cultures, religions, and countries.

During the reign of Edward I of England, seven hundred years ago, eggs were boiled, stained (dyed), covered with gold leaf, and then given as gifts to members of the royal household. And in Russia, during the time of the Czars, a jeweler by the name of Peter Carl Fabergé made the elaborate egg famous. Fabergé believed that giving an egg was

Fabergé-type Egg

the most sincere way a person could express feelings of love, admiration, and reverence. His "surprise" eggs were made of gold, silver, and crystal and set with precious jewels, and opened up to reveal an enchanting miniature. They were so fabulous that today when one of those rare eggs turns up, it sells for thousands of dollars.

Also in Russia, as well as Poland and the Ukraine, some of the most famous folk-art eggs were originated. Pysanka, as they are called, are patiently created using a wax-resist and dye method. Similar eggs, using many of the same designs, are also made in Czechoslovakia. But the Czech people create their beautiful eggs with paint and a fine-pointed brush.

Pysanka Egg

German people, too, became well known for their variety of decorated eggs. And it was the early Pennsylvania German settlers, later known as the Pennsylvania Dutch, who first introduced this craft to America. The now famous egg tree, originated during the Civil War era, is also of Pennsylvania Dutch origin. In many areas of our country, an egg-decorated tree or branch is as important at Easter as a decorated evergreen tree is at Christmas.

There is a great deal of history, and an abundant amount of information about eggs and egg decorating that you will want to read, as well as interesting stories and a variety of games. For this reason you will find a list of books, booklets, and leaflets on page 124. There is also a list of suppliers (page 125) which includes places you can purchase a variety of blown and cut shells.

First you decorate one egg, then you decorate another. After that you'll be hooked because you'll want to go on working, experimenting and creating with eggs. So let *Egg Craft* be the beginning of your lifetime hobby.

Materials and Tools

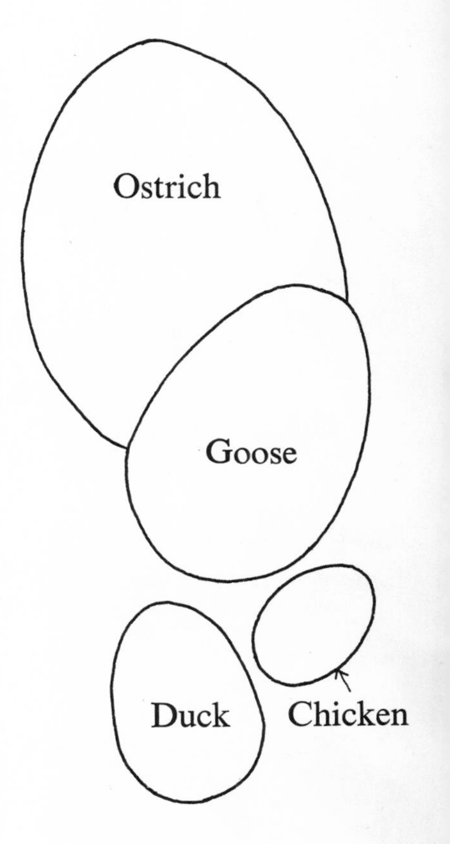

The following list is a general guide to help you find and select your materials and tools. You will not need every item on this list. Use materials you can find around your home or supplies you already have on hand. Make substitutions for those you don't. Rickrack may be substituted for fancy braid and often for ribbon. Beads can take the place of sequins, and sequins can be substituted for fake jewels. Eggers have an uncanny ability for using "found" materials and unusual items to decorate their eggs and to make egg stands. Purchase only those materials that are absolutely necessary for completing your egg projects. Also, from the suggested list of paints, choose the type of paint you have on hand or the one you prefer to work with most.

Now gather together the items you find and keep them organized in a box. Food storage boxes and shoe boxes made of plastic are excellent for storing supplies because you can see what is inside.

EGGS—Fresh chicken or duck eggs hard-boiled according to requirements of individual projects.

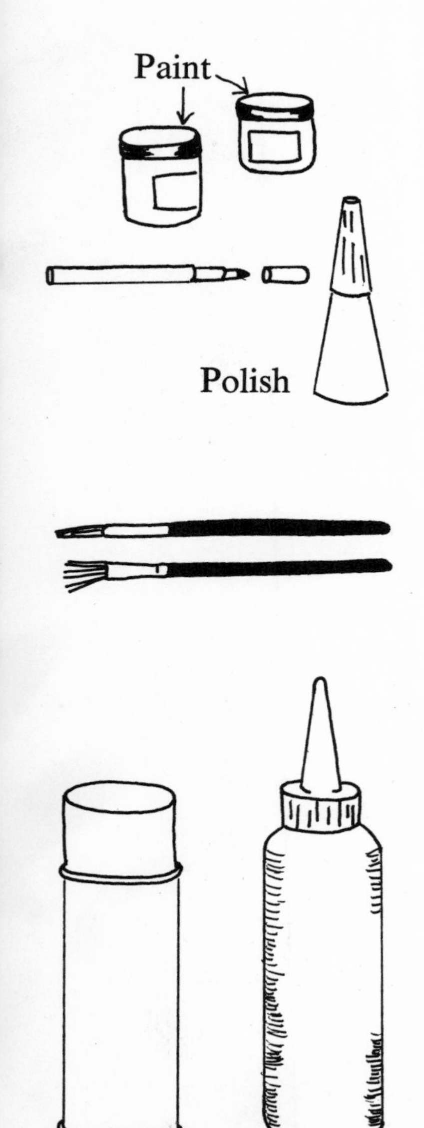

EGG SHELLS—Blown or cut. If the eggs used for cooking and baking in your home are blown instead of cracked open (see "How to Blow out Eggs," page 21), your collection of shells will grow in no time. If turkey or goose eggs are available to you, by all means include them.

PAINTS—Acrylics in jars, water-base ceramic stains (which are also acrylic), poster paints, fingernail polish (assorted colors), egg dyes, waterproof felt markers including a black marker with an extra-fine point.

PAINTBRUSHES—Assorted sizes to be used for paint, glue, and brush-on fixatives. Small fine-grain synthetic sponges and plastic foam rubber can also be used for applying paint.

FIXATIVES—Polymer medium—gloss or matt—(available at art supply and craft shops); gloss or matt varnish-like finish (spray or brush-on type); colorless nail polish.

ADHESIVES—Clear-drying, white liquid glue such as Sobo and Quik, clear-drying epoxy. There is now available in craft and hardware stores a five-minute epoxy which is excellent for egg craft.

NATURAL MATERIALS—Onion skins (save the dry, paper-like shells in a large plastic bag), a small potato, single flowers such as buttercups, violets, tiny pansies, plus grasses, ferns, and small leaves.

TRIMMINGS—Sequins, beads, pearls (all kinds such as those molded together in a string available by the yard, or those sold in long strands), flat-back paste-on jewels (broken or discarded jewelry is a good source for some of these trimmings), bell-cap jewelry findings, lace, braid, narrow ribbon, rickrack, paper lace doilies, paste-on roly-poly eyes, plain and small-print cotton fabric scraps, glitter, diamond dust (a type of glitter that resembles sugar).

PICTURES AND PRINTS—From greeting cards, gift wrapping paper, contact paper, seed catalogs, magazines, small stick-on seals.

CARDBOARD—Pulp type from egg cartons and fresh fruit and produce containers, cardboard tubes (from wax paper, plastic wrap, paper towels, etc.).

THREADS AND STRING—Metallic gift-wrap cord, colored or metallic crochet cotton, strong sewing thread, nylon fishline.

Trimmings

Pictures and Prints

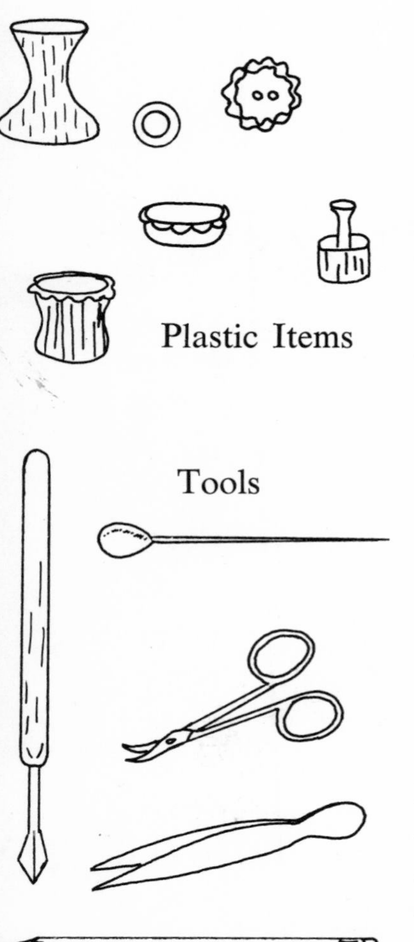

WIRE—Stem wire, coat-hanger wire, chenille stems or long pipe cleaners.

STYROFOAM—Green balls the size to fit egg used (white styrofoam may be used but must be painted).

WOODEN ITEMS—1/8 inch-diameter dowel sticks, large wooden embroidery hoop, wooden matchsticks with the heads broken off or burnt, round toothpicks.

PAPER—Tracing or tissue paper, waxed paper, construction paper or bright-colored stationery, carbon paper.

TAPE—Masking or freezer tape.

PLASTIC ITEMS—Nicely shaped and unusual bottlecaps from shampoo, lotions, cologne, etc., bone- or brass-colored curtain rings, large pretty buttons.

NYLON STOCKINGS—Old but clean.

TOOLS—Curved manicure scissors, small pair of sharp scissors, tweezers, corsage or hat pin, long thin nail, pointed skewer, or darning needle or similar pointed tool or a sgraffito knife (available from art supply, ceramic and craft shops), pencils (soft and hard), ruler, wide rubber bands, paring knife.

About Materials

EGGS—All types of eggs are used in egg craft, from tiny pullet to extra-large and jumbo chicken eggs, plus duck, goose, turkey, and pheasant eggs (but only those domestically grown).

Chicken eggs are the easiest to obtain and will probably be the kind you use most. However, if duck eggs are available in your area, you will find their slightly larger and stronger shell especially nice to work with. Other eggs, such as goose, that are used by more experienced eggers, are available at farmers' markets, egg auctions, and from farmers. Empty shells and cut-to-order shells from a variety of fowl can be purchased through the mail. (See suppliers at the back of this book.) The larger the egg, the thicker and more durable the shell. A goose egg is much thicker than a chicken egg, so cannot be cut with manicure scissors. Thick shells are emptied using a small drill bit and are cut with a jeweler's saw or a special cutting tool.

Types of eggs used in *Egg Craft* fall into three categories: blown, cut and hard-cooked. You will use blown eggs for most projects in this book. Cut eggs are shells with window-like openings cut into them. These eggs are used for several types of eggs such as diorama. Hard-cooked eggs are used for a variety of techniques including the Pennsylvania Dutch scratch-carved eggs. These eggs are not made to be eaten. Eggers rarely decorate eggs for eating but instead make eggs for their collections, display, sale, gifts, and as ornaments for egg and Christmas trees. The hard-cooked egg inside the shell will, over a period of several years, dry up into a tiny ball that will rattle when the egg is shaken.

Care must be taken when storing and handling cooked eggs because if they are broken before the contents disintegrate, the odor is overwhelming.

First-laid tiny pullet eggs are used as is. They rarely contain much yolk, so dry up easily. These tiny eggs make lovely ornaments for miniature egg trees, for earrings, or for hanging inside larger diorama eggs. Larger pullet eggs should have contents removed.

Although you will often find a variety of wild bird and fowl eggs in an egger's collection, an egger will *never* rob a nest. This is a rigid and strictly kept law among egg decorators. Whole birds' eggs can sometimes be found on the ground under trees. Robber birds or animals such as squirrels often push eggs from the nest. A collection of birds' eggs—if come by honestly—is a delight to own. However, until the contents dry up, it is wise to keep birds' eggs in a cool place. If subject to heat or sunlight, they often burst open.

PAINTS—Although poster paints can be used for egg painting they are not waterproof, so *must* be finished with a final coat of fixative. Liquid acrylic paints that come in jars are much more satisfactory. They are easy to use, thin, and clean up with water, and are permanent and waterproof when dry. Acrylics do not require a fixative, but one should be used to give depth and added shine to the paint and add more strength to the shell. Acrylic paints can be purchased at art supply and craft shops. If you do not have one of these stores near you, check your phonebook for a ceramic studio. There is usually one in even the remotest area. Water-base ceramic stains (there are many different brands), sold at ceramic studios, are also acrylic and are a joy to use for egg decorating. Not only are they available in a variety of opaque colors, but many brands come in water-base fluorescents, metallics, and pearls. Ceramic stains can usually be purchased in starter kits which include an assortment of colors. Use either a spray or brush-on fixative compatible to the brand of ceramic stain you purchase. And always remember to wash brushes immediately after use with soap and water. Once dry, acrylic paints are impossible to remove from brushes without a special brush cleaner.

Waterproof felt markers are the quick, fun way to paint designs on the plain egg. A black fine-line felt marker is also a must for outlining painted designs if you wish to duplicate folk-type eggs. (Pen and India ink may be substituted for the black marker.)

Colored nail polish is a good substitute for lacquer paints which many advanced eggers use when making elaborate, jeweled Fabergé-type eggs. Nail polish is used when an egg is to be trimmed with beads, fake jewels, or similar trimmings. Colored nail polish is *not* for painting freehand designs. Colorless nail polish is an excellent fixative for poster paints and dyed eggs. It dries hard and adds strength to the shell.

Brown eggs as well as hard-cooked eggs may be dyed with Easter-egg dyes. Such shells make good plain eggs that can be used as the basic egg for many projects.

When painting or dyeing eggs, you will find it helpful to have a collection of props to keep eggs safe and secure as they dry. These props can be jar lids, eggcups, stem wire, or anything else you can dream up.

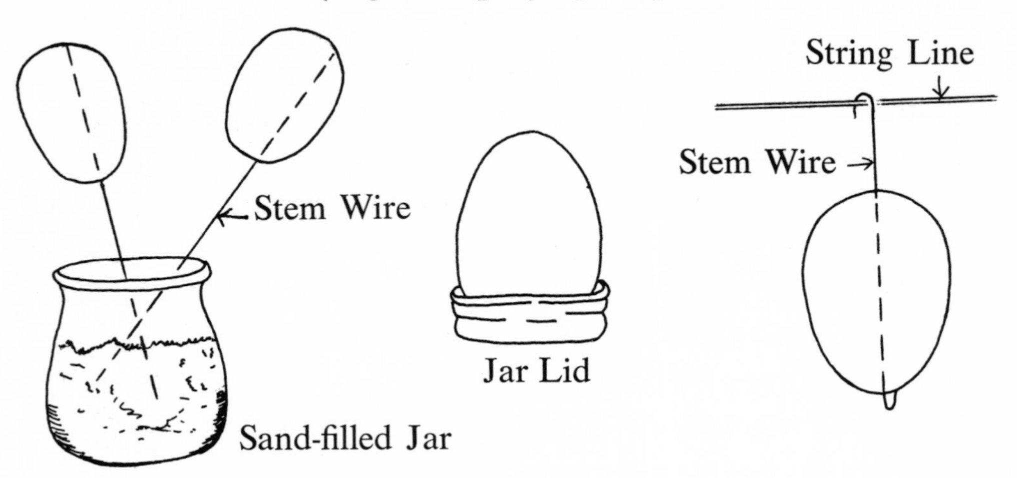

FIXATIVES—A fixative is a clear final coat put on after the egg is complete or whenever directions instruct its use. Some are brush-on and some are spray-on. Some give a glossy shine while others produce a satin-like finish.

Fixatives are used to seal paint, add depth and shine, and to protect surface from soil. For most egg projects two coats of fixative are sufficient. Always be sure to allow time for the first coat to dry before applying the second.

For acrylic paints you can use polymer medium, either gloss or matt, as your fixative. This is a white milky liquid which dries clear and which has many uses besides being a fixative. To apply polymer medium, first dip your brush in clean water, removing the excess moisture by touching the brush to an absorbent paper towel, then dip it into the polymer medium. Flow the medium onto the egg as smoothly as possible to avoid brush marks. Do not dip your brush back into the water unless it absolutely must be cleaned. (Polymer medium has a tendency to pile up in the bristles.) Remember always to remove excess water from the brush each time it is cleaned. If too much water is allowed to remain in the brush, the finish may dry cloudy. Paint one half of the egg, set egg in a bottlecap or other prop, let dry, then paint the other half. The second coat should be brushed on in the same direction as the first. Wash brush immediately after use with a mild soap and water. Polymer medium is also an excellent material to use for a quick and easy form of découpage eggs.

Many spray-type fixatives are suitable for acrylic paint. The advantages of a spray fixative over brush-on are that the whole egg may be sprayed each time a coat is applied and you do not have to hold the shell in your hand. Also, spray-on fixatives give an even, glass-like coat which is lovely. To use spray-on fixatives, spear the blown shell on a stiff wire and spray. If you hold the egg in your hand, you will find that your fingers will stick to the shell and when removed, some of the painted surface will be pulled away. For eggs without holes, prop eggs in a jar lid, spray one half, let dry, turn egg over and spray the other half.

Poster paints and dyed eggs may be finished with colorless nail polish, polymer medium, clear plastic spray, or some spray fixatives. It is always wise to test fixatives for all paints by first brushing some paint spots on a piece of cardboard or broken egg shell, letting paint dry, then spraying to be sure fixative is compatible with the paint and will not cause it to bleed.

Many ceramic stains have their own brush-on fixatives or sealers. Most of these products are similar to polymer medium and are applied in the same way. However, spray fixatives are generally used for ceramic stains.

An excellent spray fixative which is widely available in art supply, craft, and ceramic shops is Blair Spray-Clear. It can safely be used over most painted and other surfaces.

For découpage, if you prefer a spray finish to a brush-on, you will find many brands available. Always remember to seal egg and prints with two coats of a fixative before using a découpage finish.

ADHESIVES—Both Sobo and Quik are white liquid, clear-drying glues. Both are excellent products and if used properly will hold items fast. Never use great globs of glue or more glue than is necessary to paste materials together. On the other hand, be sure to use enough or trimmings and such will eventually fall off the egg surface.

Quik is thicker than Sobo and is used whenever you want something to grab hold fast, like beads and jewels. Sobo is best when a thin, smooth layer or line of glue is desired. Use it for gluing paper cutouts or glitter.

For a neat, clean job, apply Sobo and Quik with an inexpensive paintbrush or toothpick in fine lines for braids and laces or in dots when attaching beads.

Epoxy is used only when Sobo or Quik cannot do the job, such as sticking metal to metal, plastics to metal, or for other non-porous materials.

TRIMMINGS—Some braids and trimmings today are self-adhesive and will require no glue. When using these trimmings, peel off paper backing and stick trimming on the shell. Tiny trimmings such as beads, sequins, and small shell pieces will be easier to handle and place on egg if you use tweezers instead of your fingers, or if you create a toothpick tool as described on page 105, Beaded Eggs.

Ends of metallic trimmings often fray. This problem can be eliminated if you brush ends with colorless nail polish. Let nail polish dry before using.

Special Instructions

How to Blow out Eggs

Begin with fresh, room-temperature eggs. Never use eggs directly from the refrigerator. Cold eggs are difficult to blow.

Use a hat pin or corsage pin to pierce a hole in one end of the egg (usually the large end). You may find this easier to do if you tap the pin *gently* with a knife handle (Fig. 1). Next make a hole in the other end. Enlarge this hole by carefully breaking away bits of the shell with the point of the pin (Fig. 2). Keep hole as small as possible, about ¼ inch in diameter, never any larger unless directions tell you otherwise. Another method of enlarging the hole uses a small pair of *sharp*, pointed scissors. Insert tip of one scissor's blade in the hole, then *slowly, carefully,* and *gently* turn blade around and around in the hole (Fig. 3). When done successfully, this method will give you a nice round, clean-edged hole.

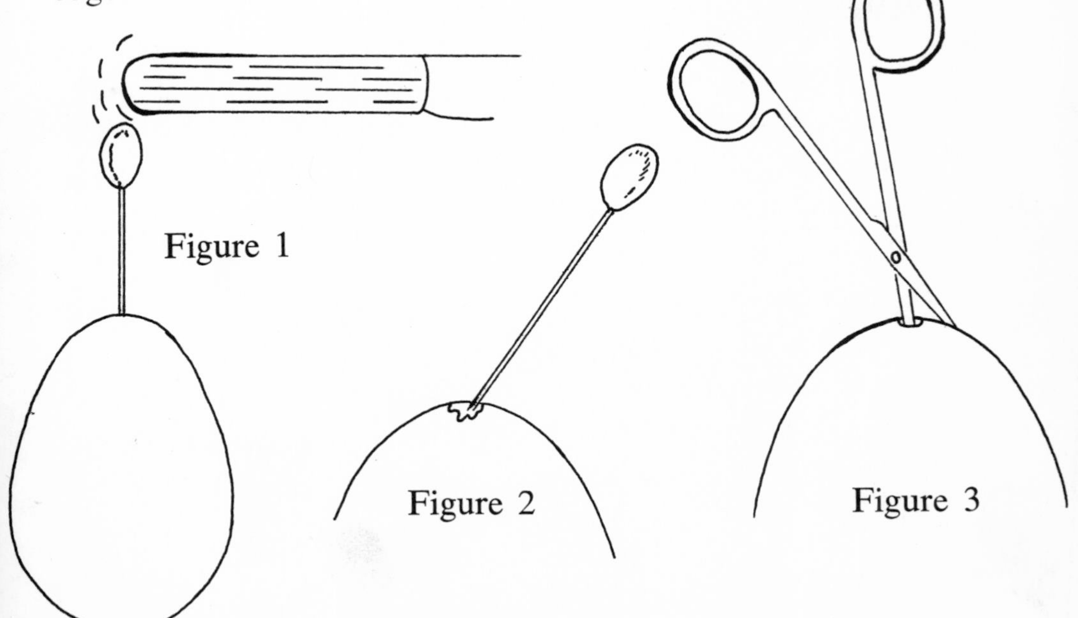

Figure 1

Figure 2

Figure 3

Now, push pin inside the egg, pierce, break, then stir the yolk well. Put your finger over the holes and shake the egg vigorously to scramble the contents. Thoroughly breaking up the yolk will make blowing easier. Hold egg over a bowl. Blow through the small hole to force the egg out the large hole. The first egg you blow will seem difficult, the second a little easier, and by the time you have done a dozen, you'll consider yourself a professional.

Immediately after emptying, rinse the shell out with water, then prop it on paper towels or an egg carton to air-dry.

If your mother or another female adult decides to help you blow eggs, be sure she removes her lipstick. Grease in lipstick will later prevent paint from adhering to the shell.

Blown shells can be safely stored for a long time in egg cartons, baskets, and large plastic containers.

The raw egg contents should immediately be stored in a covered container and put in the refrigerator. They should be used within twenty-four hours for cooking or baking.

If you intend to display your finished eggs in a basket and stand and will not be covering the holes with beads or other trimmings, cover them with paper when the shells are thoroughly dry. Cut small circles from thin white paper slightly larger than the hole in the egg. Apply a thin line of glue around the edge of the hole and stick a paper circle over it; let dry. Tear excess paper away so that the torn edges of circle will blend into the egg shell (Fig. 1). You need only cover the enlarged holes. Tiny pinholes usually fill up with paint.

Tear Excess Paper Away.

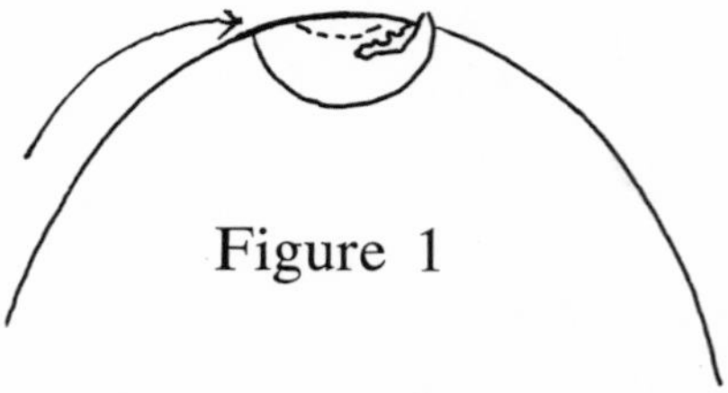

Figure 1

How to Cut Eggs
To cut a window-like opening in a shell for a diorama, start with a fresh egg. Draw the shape of the window on the shell with pencil (Fig. 1). This will be easier to do if you use a paper pattern to trace around. Pierce a hole in the center of the window with a corsage or hat pin. Enlarge hole by breaking away tiny bits of the shell until it is large enough to empty out the raw contents (Fig. 2). Now, with curved manicure scissors, cut around and around the hole (Fig. 3), until the window is cut to the size and shape drawn (Fig. 4).

Cutting eggs with manicure scissors will seem impossible at first, but once you master the technique you'll discover it is not as difficult to do as you thought it would be. There are several precautions which must be taken as you cut. Nip off only small bits of the shell with scissors. Don't try to bite off large chunks or cut directly to your penciled line. You must work slowly and hold the egg gently but firmly, turning it as you cut. Feed the shell deep into the scissor's blades, but don't close the blade points, as this causes cracks and breaks.

Some eggers feel it is easier to cut a shell when it is fresh.

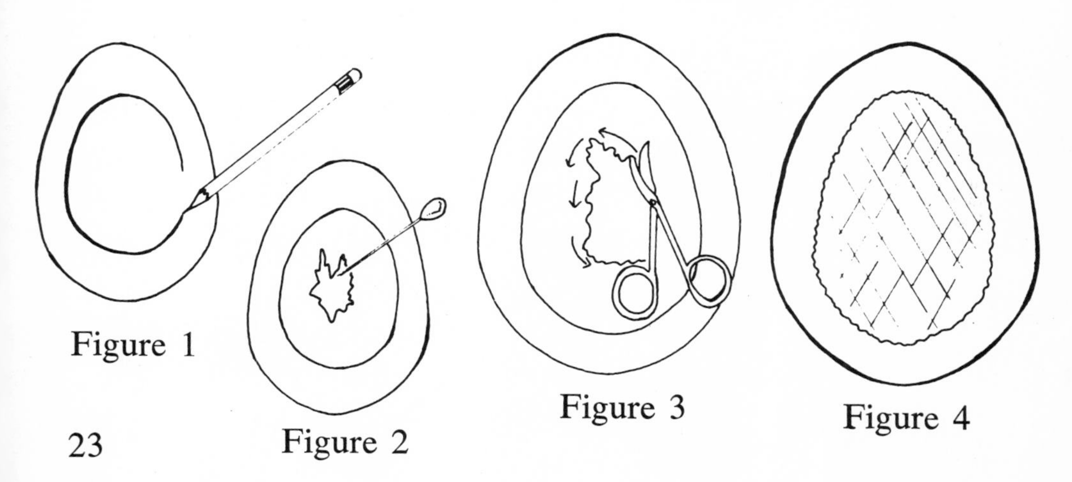
Figure 1
Figure 2
Figure 3
Figure 4

Others say it is better to blow the egg and then let the shell stand a few days before cutting it. Still others paint over the drawn pencil line with glue, let glue dry, then cut the egg. The glue sometimes helps to prevent cracks. You could try all these methods and decide which one works best for you. Eggers always experiment to find what methods and techniques suit them best. Don't be discouraged if you are not successful at first.

If the edges of the opening are ragged and if tiny cracks appear around the edge, do not become upset. Paint, especially acrylic types, will fill and hold cracks together, and trimmings will cover and hide ragged edges.

Don't forget to wash out the shell and remove the loose layer of membrane, then rinse shell again and allow it to dry.

If you find that you have done a particularly fine job of cutting a window but several bad hairline cracks appear in the shell, try this remedy for saving your egg. Brush outside shell with a layer of glue. Sprinkle shell glitter (see page 25), on the wet glue so that the shell is completely covered. When glue is dry, carefully paint the inside of the egg with a pastel-colored nail polish and your egg will be as good as new.

How to Handle Egg Shells

The first thing you must learn when handling an egg shell is not to be afraid of it. Egg shells are fragile. If you drop one it will break, but it is amazing how much pressure a shell will take from your fingers before it cracks.

Always hold a shell firmly but gently while working or painting on it. How firmly is something that cannot be taught or shown; it is something you must learn yourself.

With each coat of paint and fixative, the shell becomes

stronger. The egg will withstand a lot of handling and admiring so long as a certain amount of care is taken. However, the finished egg is not unbreakable and will crack if dropped or bumped sharply. This is why eggers, when packing eggs for any reason, wrap them in cotton or shredded foam rubber and put them in strong metal containers.

If, when you are blowing, cutting, or working on an egg, the shell breaks, don't be discouraged. Instead, save the pieces. Partial shells can often become baskets or tulips, and pieces can make mosaics (see Mosaic Flower, page 103). In fact, a great many artists use egg shells to create mosaic murals, paintings, jewelry trays and boxes. Egg-shell art is a craft all by itself. Also, with broken shells—plain or colored, or a mixture of both—you can make your own brand of glitter. Put pieces of shells in a small plastic bag. Roll a rolling pin over the bag until the shells are crushed very fine. Use this glitter to cover the outside or inside of diorama eggs or whenever you wish to add a different touch to any plain egg.

Handling and decorating eggs require patience, the ability to resign yourself to breaks when they come, a firm but gentle hand, and a lot of fortitude. But every minute spent decorating eggs will be well worth the time and effort.

Methods of Hanging Eggs

There are a variety of ways in which ribbon, fishing line, or threads can be attached to an egg so that it can be suspended from a tree branch, in a window, or anywhere you please. Here are some of them.

1. Tie a long length of narrow ribbon, cord, or thread to

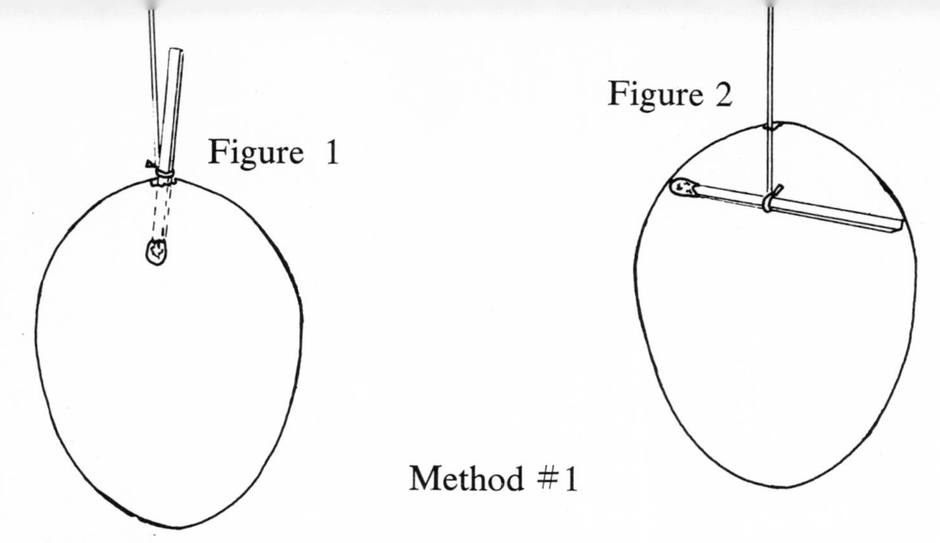

the middle of a wooden matchstick. A bit of glue around the stick where the thread is tied will keep it from slipping. Carefully insert matchstick straight down into largest egg hole (Fig. 1). The stick will become wedged crosswise inside the shell and will not pull out (Fig. 2). This method is excellent for making mobiles.

2. Fold a long length of ribbon in half. Tie ends together in a bow or square knot (Fig. 1). Bend one end of a piece of stem wire over to make a very skinny U-shape (Fig. 2). Push the U-end of the wire through the top hole in the egg and out the bottom hole. Catch the loop end of the ribbon in the bend of the wire and pull the ribbon through the egg (Fig. 3). Tie a knot in the ribbon right at the top of the egg (Fig. 4).

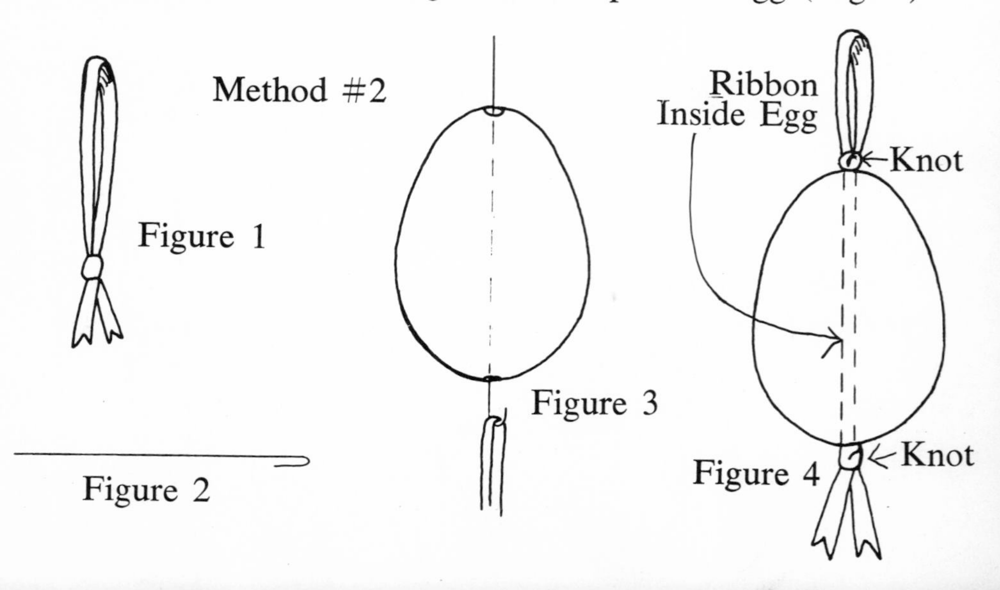

This method will require both holes in the egg to be large enough to accommodate the width of the ribbon used, but not so large that the ribbon pulls through the egg.

3. This method is almost like the one above, but uses large, pretty beads and fine cord or crochet cotton. Fold a long length of cord in half. Either knot ends together or tie a small bead to the cord ends. The cord used must be fine enough to fit through bead hole, yet strong enough to support the egg. String some fancy beads on the cord, then pull the cord through the egg using the U-end stem wire. Add some beads at the top and knot the cord just above the last bead.

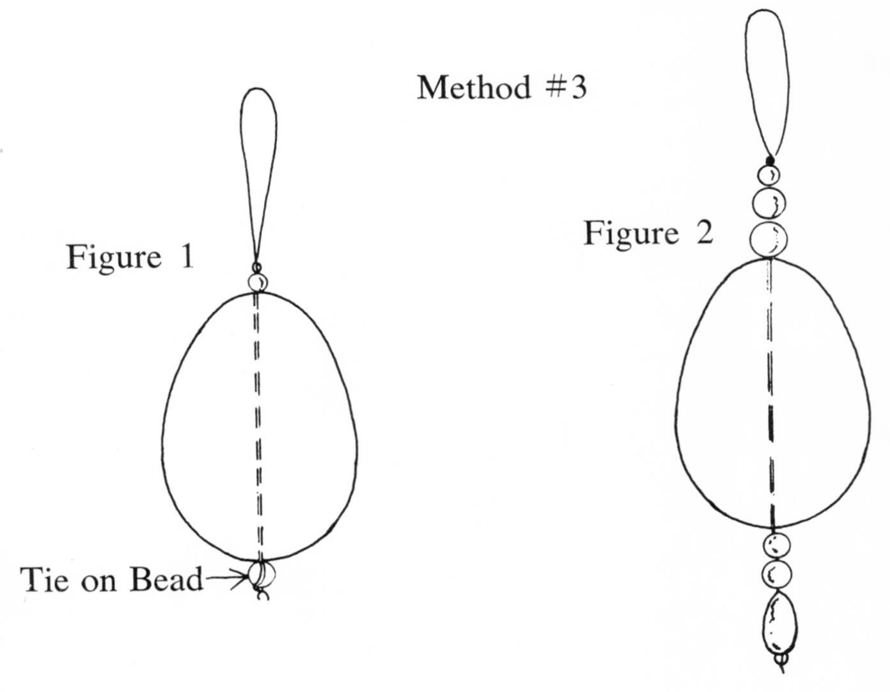

4. Available from craft shops and mail-order houses is a variety of jewelry findings, such as bell caps and up-eyes, that can be cemented to the top of eggs. These caps are best

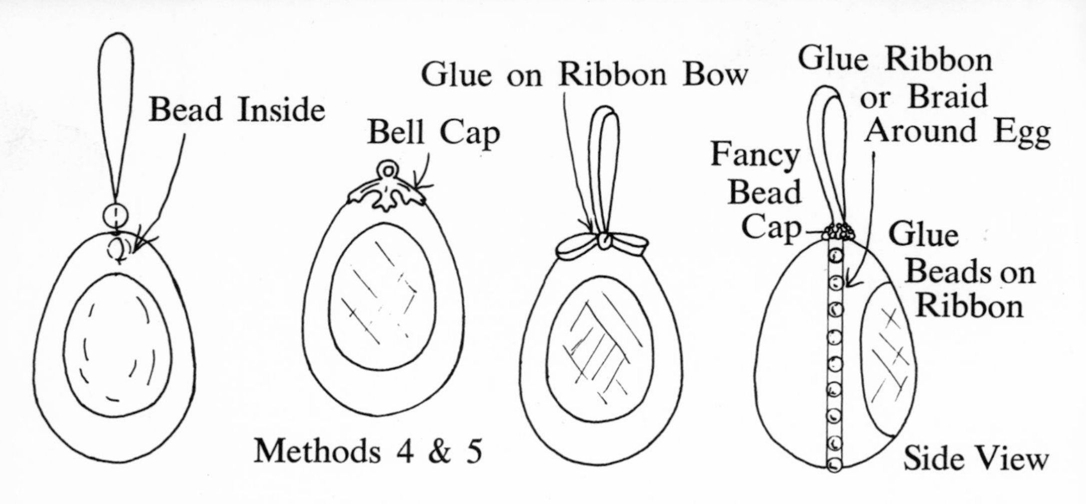

cemented in place with epoxy or a jewelry cement, especially if the egg is to hang. A cord or thread loop is put through the hole in the bell cap for hanging.

5. Bell caps can also be used to hang diorama eggs. Or you may use any one of the methods shown.

Stands for Eggs

It will be surprising how many items you will find around your home that will make delightful egg stands. Fancy bottle caps, curtain rings, candleholders, buttons, eggcups, a cardboard ring, an eggcup from an egg carton are just some of the things you can use. With a little imagination, some paint, a combination of items and possibly the addition of beads and trimmings, a collection of stands is easy to acquire.

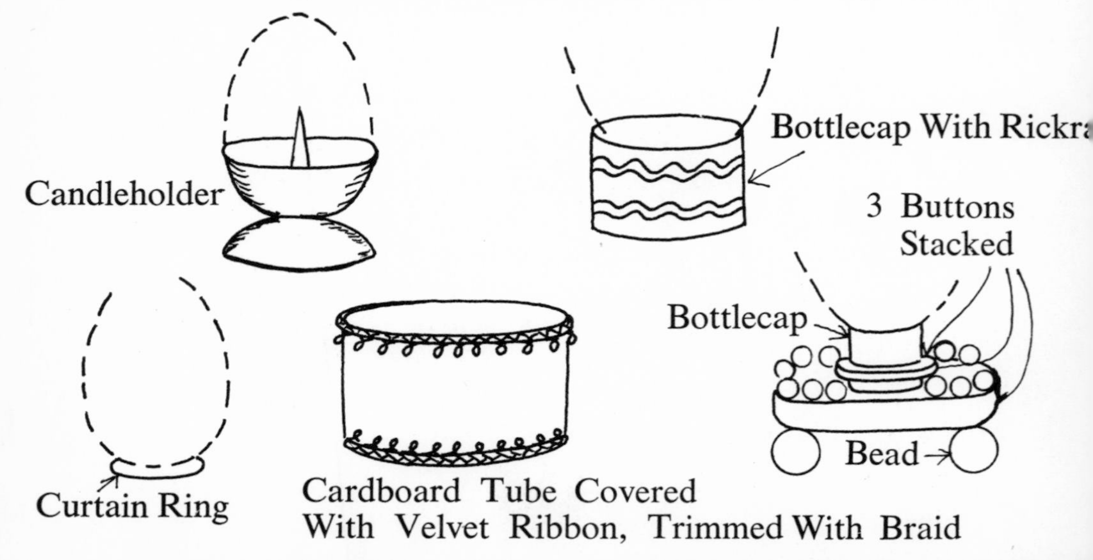

Of course there are many stands available from craft shops and mail-order houses. A few are very expensive and are generally used by eggers for their elaborate egg creations.

How to Shape Pulp Cardboard

The pulp-paper cardboard used to make egg cartons and fresh fruit and vegetable containers is great material for such things as wings on bird eggs and ears on bunny eggs. The cardboard can be shaped, curled, and bent easily if you follow these steps.

1. Cut desired shapes—wings, ears, leaves, etc.—from egg-carton lids or other pulp cardboard containers.
2. Place the flat shapes in a bowl of warm water for 3 to 4 minutes. Shapes will float on the surface of the water, so be sure to turn them over often and push them under the water occasionally so that they become evenly saturated.
3. Remove a shape and carefully mold it to the form you want, or however instructions tell you. If the cardboard cracks badly, it needs to be soaked in water a little longer. If it is mushy or crumbles, it has been soaking too long. When it is just right, tiny cracks and tears can be repaired by simply dipping a finger in water and pressing the cardboard back together again.
4. Set shapes aside to dry on absorbent paper towels. Reshape them occasionally as they dry. Then proceed with the next step of the instructions for the egg you are making.

Tracing and Transferring Designs and Patterns

To Trace—Lay a piece of tracing paper or white tissue paper just slightly larger than needed over the pattern or design. Hold it in place with paper clips. Draw over all lines carefully with a soft black pencil. Remove tracing.

To Transfer a Design to a Plain Egg—Turn design tracing over to the wrong side. Draw over all lines again with a soft black pencil. (When complete, both sides of the paper will have a penciled design.) Lay tracing on egg, holding it in place with small pieces of masking tape. Go over all lines of the design with a hard pencil to transfer the design to the egg. Be sure you have drawn on all lines before removing the tracing. Never use carbon paper to transfer designs to eggs, as it will leave black smudges on the painted shell.

To Transfer Patterns to Pulp Cardboard or Stiff Paper—Use carbon paper. Place it shiny side down on the cardboard; put tracing on top. Hold them all in place with masking tape, then go over all lines with a hard pencil.

How to Make Frosting

With the following recipe you can simulate frosting or snow in diorama scenes or add textured designs to eggs.

This recipe will make approximately enough frosting for two make-believe sugar eggs. If stored in a tightly covered container, it will keep for several days.

1½ tablespoons cornstarch
¼ teaspoon liquid white glue
2 tablespoons white paint (acrylic or ceramic stain)

Combine the above ingredients in a small plastic container and mix throughly. The mixture should be the consistency of fluffy frosting and be able to hold peaks. If too thin, sprinkle in a little more cornstarch. If too thick, add a few drops of water. Keep container covered when not working with the frosting; if it is exposed to the air too long, it will dry out and become hard.

Displaying Eggs

Every egger displays eggs in his or her home all year round. Some are hung from curtain rods or ceilings; others are arranged on shelves and window sills, or in cabinets with glass doors. Baskets or dishes of eggs will be found on tables, and extra-special eggs are usually found under glass domes. Eggers are proud of their creations and want to show them off.

Probably the most popular method of displaying eggs (for non-eggers also) is the egg tree. In many homes Easter would not be Easter without this tree, but in most eggers' homes an egg tree is on display at all times.

An egg tree can be as large or as small as you wish. It can be a small branch cut from a spring flowering shrub or it can be a large manzanita branch purchased from a craft shop. The only requirement an egg tree should have is lots of little branches strong enough to hold eggs.

An egg tree can be set permanently into a container by filling the container with plaster of Paris. Or it can be made a temporary thing by using sand and rocks to fill the container you select. This container can be anything from a vase to a crock or a plastic paint bucket to a large round tub. It should, however, be large enough and heavy enough to support securely the size branch or tree you have chosen.

Eggs on constant display will become dusty. To clean and dust them, use a small, soft, barely damp cloth or soft-bristle paintbrushes.

The Plain Egg

A plain egg is a solid-color egg shell. Almost every egg project in this book will begin with a plain egg. There are several methods for getting color or paint onto the shells.

How to Paint

With Brush—The only drawback about painting eggs with a brush is that you can do only one half of the egg. Then you have to let the paint dry, before you do the other half. When a brush is used to apply paint, a lap line sometimes occurs where you stopped on the first half and started on the second half. Rather than ending the first half of your egg with a straight line, end it with a staggered, feathered line. Then when you paint the second half you can blend the paint into the first half. Always apply paint as smoothly as possible and watch out for brush strokes. Two coats of paint will be required for good coverage.

With Sponge—Applying paint with a fine-grain, soft sponge has many advantages. There are never lap lines or brush strokes and you get a nice even coverage. If you should have to touch up the color later, it will not show. To apply paint with a sponge, first rinse sponge in clean water, then squeeze it between several paper towels to remove excess moisture. The sponge should be barely damp. Put about a tablespoon of paint in a jar lid, then dip sponge into the paint. The sponge should be filled but not dripping. Lightly dab paint on one half of the egg. Don't worry if there are any bare spots showing. Let the paint dry, then sponge the other half of the egg. Put more paint in the lid and repeat with several more coats until egg is solidly covered. Remember to wash the sponge with soap and water immediately after using. Note: When you want a white plain egg, paint it white, even though the egg you use is white to begin with. Besides giving it a brighter, more even white, the paint will strengthen the shell.

With Dyes—Blown, cut, cooked eggs and those broken shells you have been saving may be dyed with Easter egg dyes. Follow directions on dye package for mixing and use.

Because they are so light, blown eggs will float in the dye water. For an even coverage of color, turn egg over often and spoon dye over the shell. Or force shell under the dye until it fills and sinks to the bottom of the container, making sure the dye water is deep enough to cover the whole shell.

A variety of natural materials, such as onion skins, can be used for dyeing eggs (see Pennsylvania Dutch Scratch-carved Eggs and English Pace Eggs). In place of the onion skins you might try spinach for a green color, coffee grounds for a brown color, and carrots for red. Dyes will adhere better if you add a few drops of vinegar to the dye bath.

With Nail Polish—This is always applied with a brush and is used in this book for beaded eggs. However, you can also use nail polish for diorama and ribbon-and-lace eggs. Nail polish comes in many lovely colors and requires no fixative.

When applying polish, flow it on smoothly to avoid brush marks. If polish seems thick, thin it with a few drops of nail-polish remover.

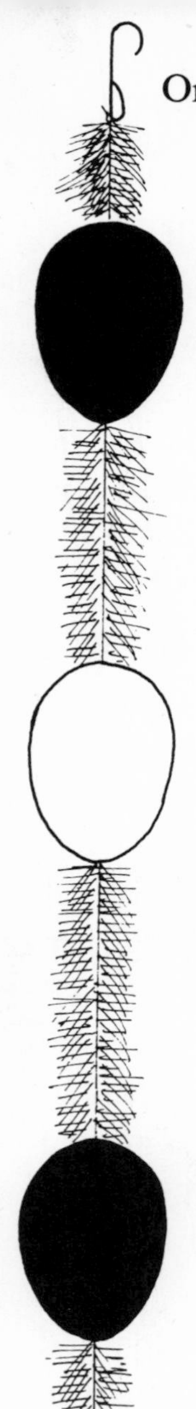

Egg Garland

You Will Need:

5 to 8 plain eggs with enlarged holes at both ends (eggs can be all one color or assorted colors)

fixative

Christmas tinsel garland, 5 or 6 feet long

2 Christmas ornament hooks

How to Make It:

1. Seal each egg with a fixative and let dry.

2. Carefully string eggs on the tinsel garland. Use your U-end stem wire (page 26) to pull the strand of tinsel through the eggs. Place them about 8 to 10 inches apart. Be sure the holes in the eggs are large enough to allow them to slide along the garland, but not so large that they won't stay where they are finally put.

3. Tie an ornament hook to each end of the finished garland to help keep it in place on the Christmas tree.

Mobile Chandelier

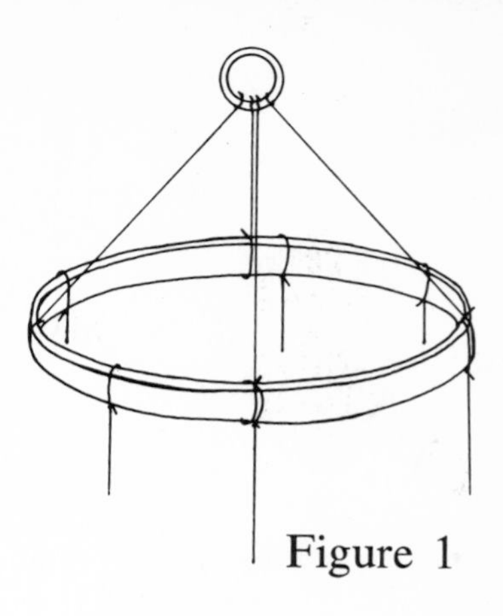

Figure 1

You Will Need:

About 7 plain eggs (number will depend on size of hoop used)
1 section of a large wooden embroidery hoop
gold-colored curtain ring
nylon fishing line or strong black thread
wooden matchsticks (1 for each egg)
fixative
scissors

How to Make It:

1. Brush or spray each egg with 2 coats of fixative. Let dry.
2. String each egg on a long thread as directed on page 25, method 1.
3. Space eggs evenly around the embroidery hoop and tie. Have some eggs hang on long threads, others on shorter threads. Save one egg for hanging later.
4. Tie 4 long threads evenly spaced around the top of the hoop. Tie the other ends of the threads to a curtain ring (Fig. 1).
5. Attach the last egg to the curtain ring so that it hangs from the ring, through the center of the hoop and lower than all the other eggs. Adjust string lengths if necessary to make mobile hang straight.

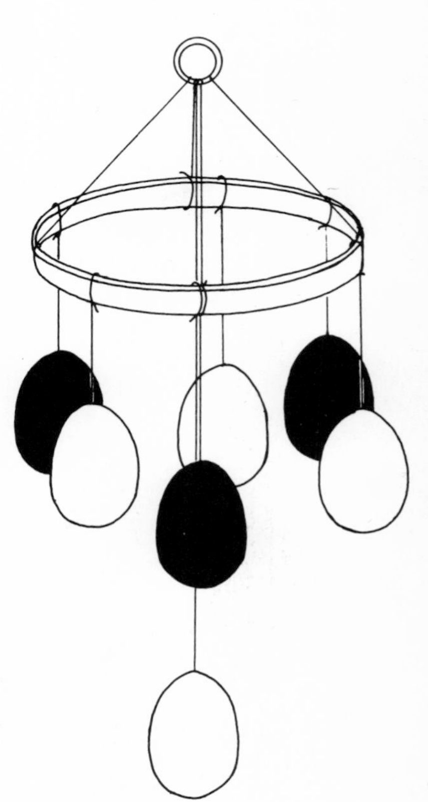

Party Candy Cup

You Will Need:

plain egg (any color)
lid from pulp-cardboard egg carton
paint, green and black
glue (Quik)
brushes (for paint and glue)
fixative
pencil, tracing and carbon paper, tweezers, scissors, bowl of warm water

How to Make It:

1. Trace and transfer leaf pattern to the egg-carton lid following directions on pages 29–30. Cut out leaf with scissors.

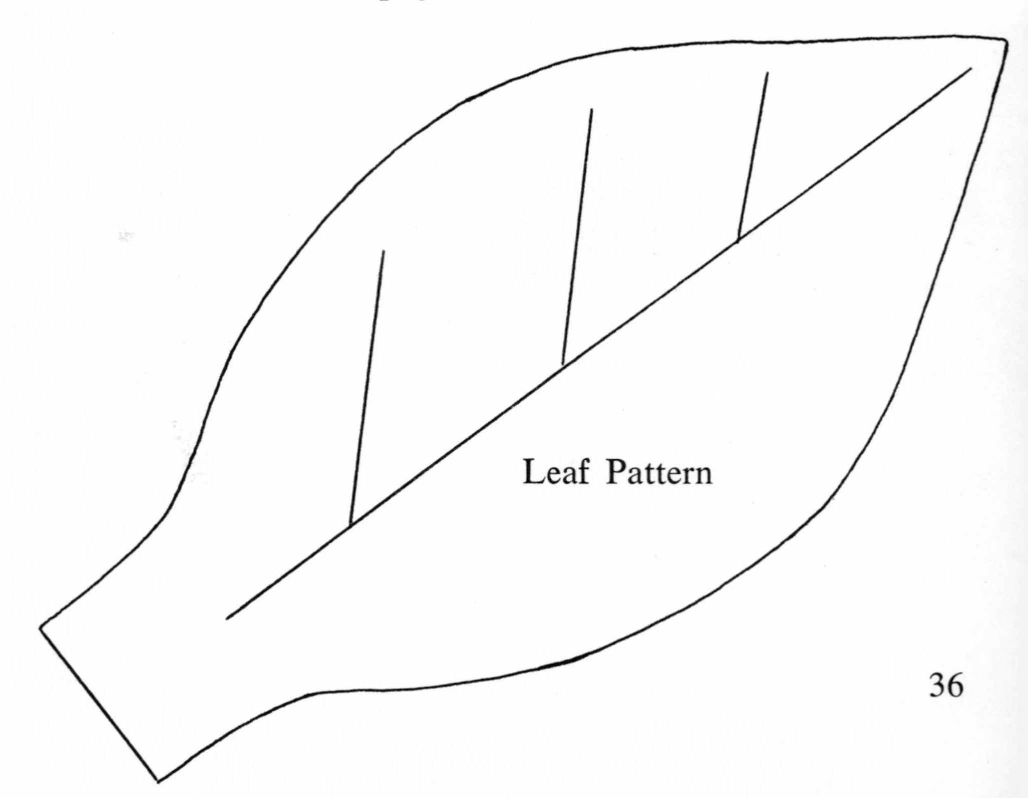

2. Soak leaf in water until it is pliable and can be shaped (see page 29). Curl leaf as desired, but shape it so that the base of the egg will sit securely near the stem end. Set leaf aside to dry.

3. To make the cup from the plain egg, use tweezers and carefully break away tiny pieces of shell at narrow end of egg (Fig. 1). Break away the top third of the egg only.

4. Paint leaf green. When dry, paint black vein lines on both sides. Glue bottom of eggcup on leaf near stem end. When glue is dry, finish egg and leaf with 2 coats of fixative. Make several candy cups for a party. Fill eggs with tiny mints, jelly beans, or other candies.

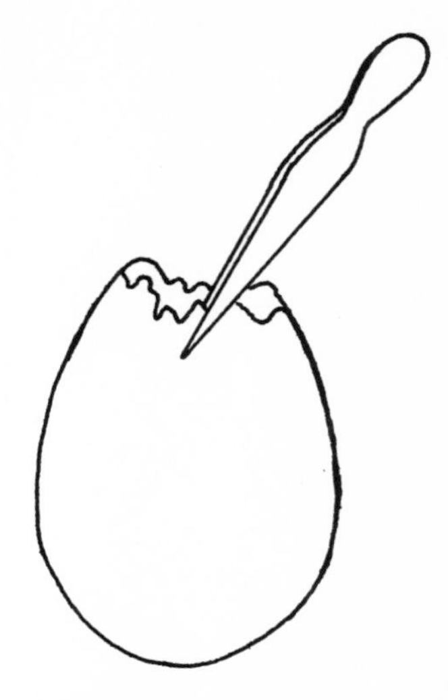

Figure 1

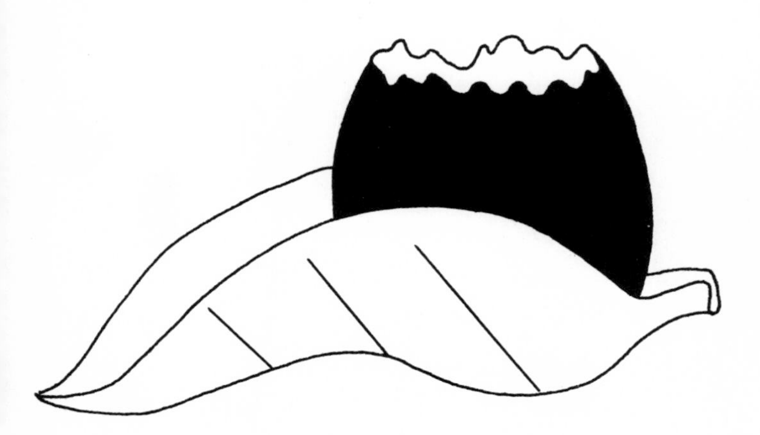

Tulips

You Will Need:

plain eggs painted tulip colors (red, yellow, purple, pink)

two 12-inch green chenille stems for each egg

glue

tweezers

fixative

artificial greens, such as plastic ferns and leaves

a vase or planter

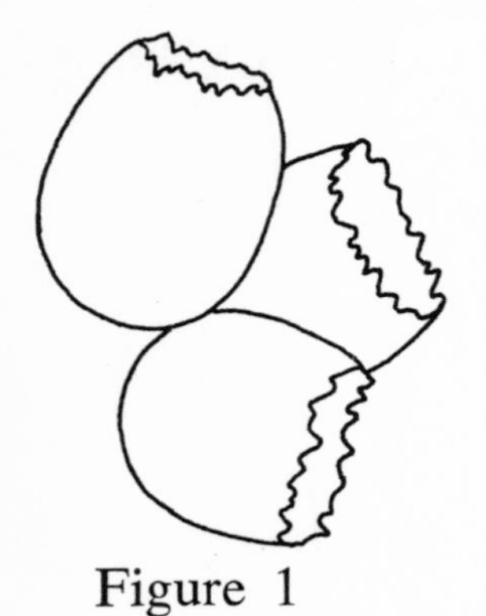

Figure 1

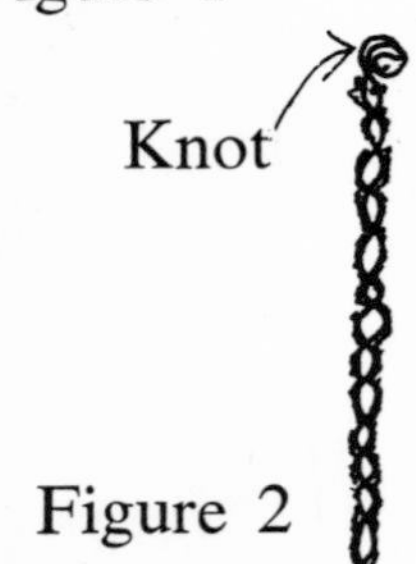

Figure 2

Stem Inside Egg

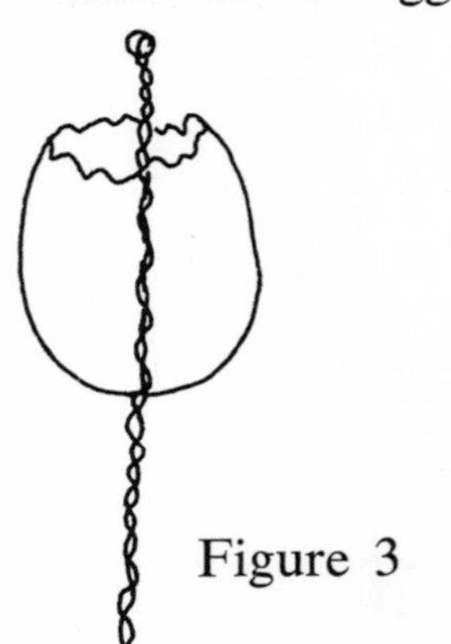

Figure 3

How to Make It:

1. Using tweezers, carefully break away small bits of shell at small end of eggs until they resemble tulips (Fig. 1). (If you accidentally broke an end off any eggs while blowing them, they could be used at this time to make tulips.) Apply 2 coats of fixative.

2. Twist 2 green chenille stems together. Twist and curl one end into a small knot-like bump (Fig. 2). Put some glue on the underside of the knot and push the stem end into the hole in the bottom of a tulip (Fig. 3). Gently pull stem all the way through tulip shell until the knot rests on the inside bottom of the shell

(Fig. 4). Let glue dry. Make several tulips in the same way.

3. Arrange tulips with artificial greens in a vase or planter.

Figure 4

Silver Bells

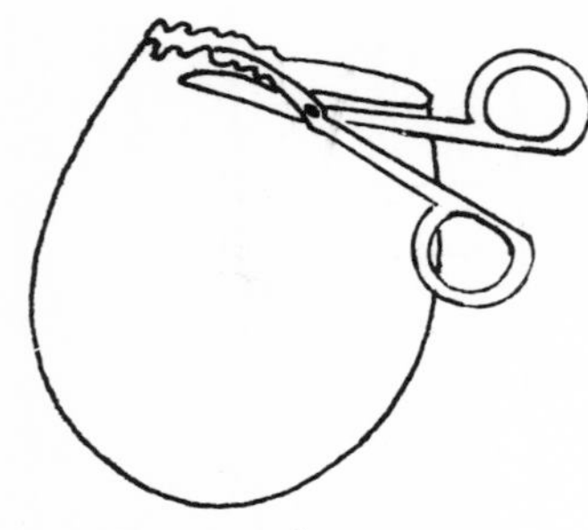

Figure 1

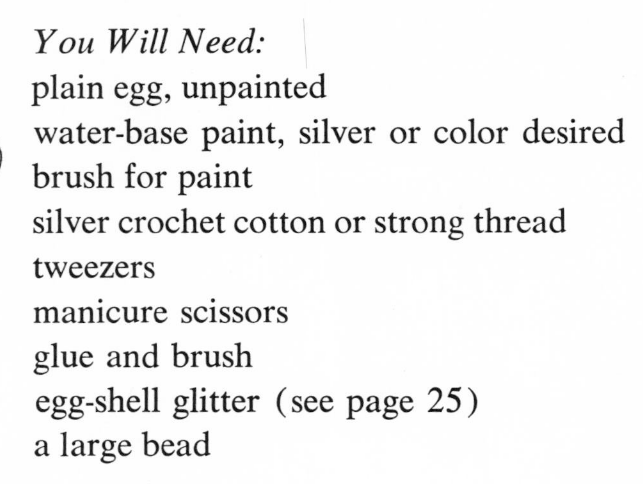

You Will Need:

plain egg, unpainted
water-base paint, silver or color desired
brush for paint
silver crochet cotton or strong thread
tweezers
manicure scissors
glue and brush
egg-shell glitter (see page 25)
a large bead

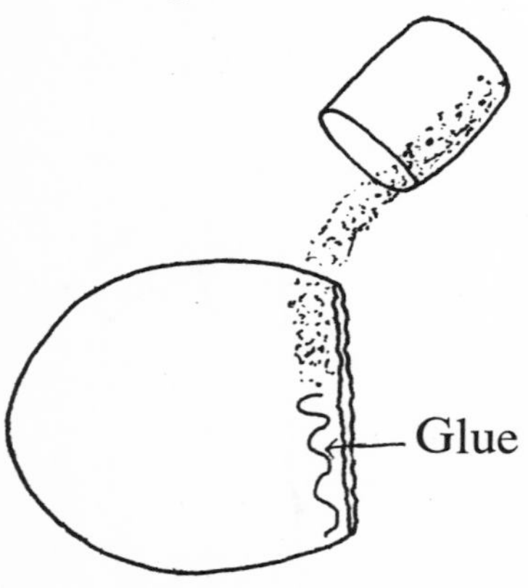

Figure 2

How to Make It:

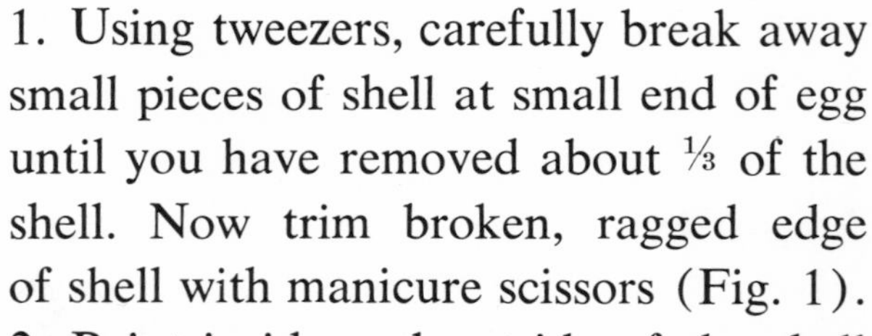

1. Using tweezers, carefully break away small pieces of shell at small end of egg until you have removed about ⅓ of the shell. Now trim broken, ragged edge of shell with manicure scissors (Fig. 1).
2. Paint inside and outside of the shell silver. Let paint dry.
3. Using a brush, paint a band of glue along the bottom edge of the egg-shell bell. Immediately sprinkle egg-shell glitter on the wet glue (Fig. 2). Let dry.
4. Fold a 7-inch piece of silver crochet cotton in half. Tie end together. This will be the hanging loop. Push folded end of the loop through hole in the bead (Fig. 3), and pull loop all the way through until knot is pulled against the

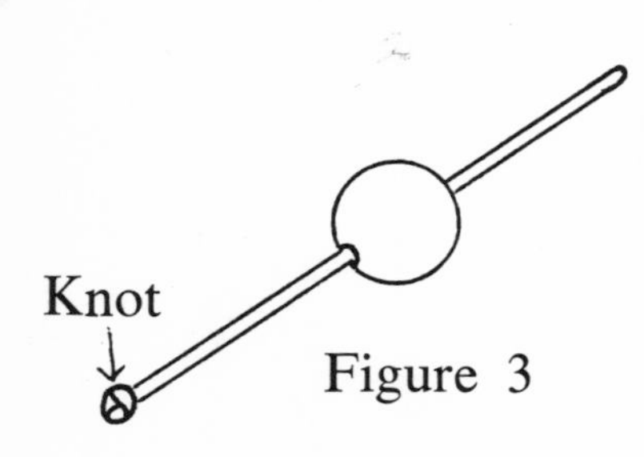

Figure 3

bead. (If using fine thread, tie bead to ends of strands.) Next, push folded end of the hanging loop inside the egg bell and through the hole in the top (Fig. 4). Pull the loop through the hole, letting bead clapper suspend from the top of the bell (Fig. 5). Make a knot in the hanging loop on the outside top of the bell shell.

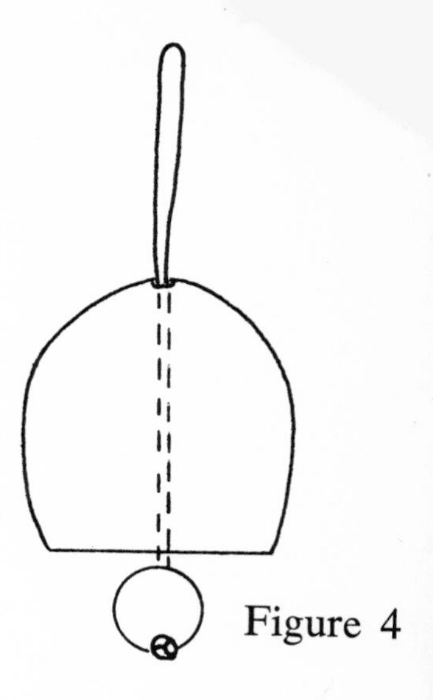

Figure 4

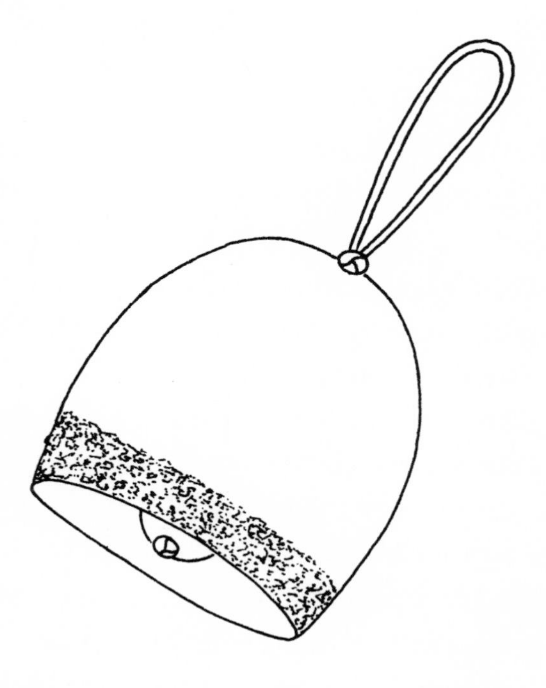

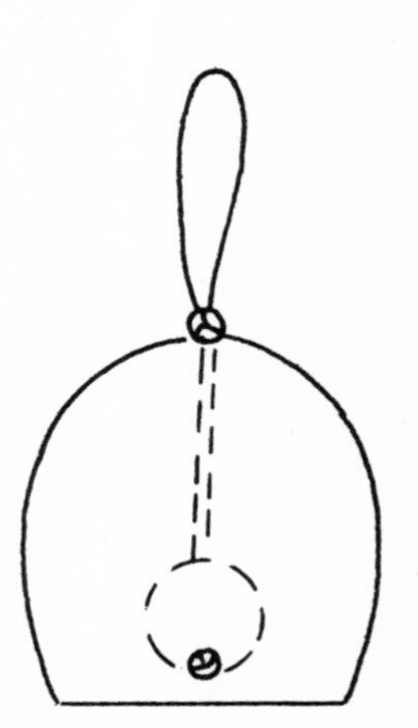

Figure 5

Basket

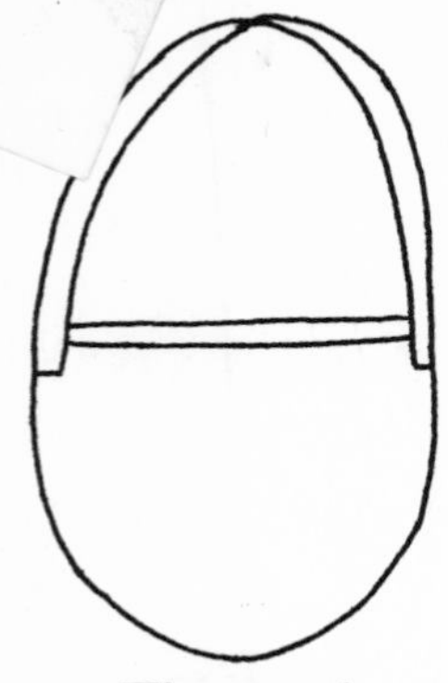
Figure 1

You Will Need:
plain egg, unpainted
paint, any color
tweezers
manicure scissors
fixative
glue and brush
narrow ribbon
scissors

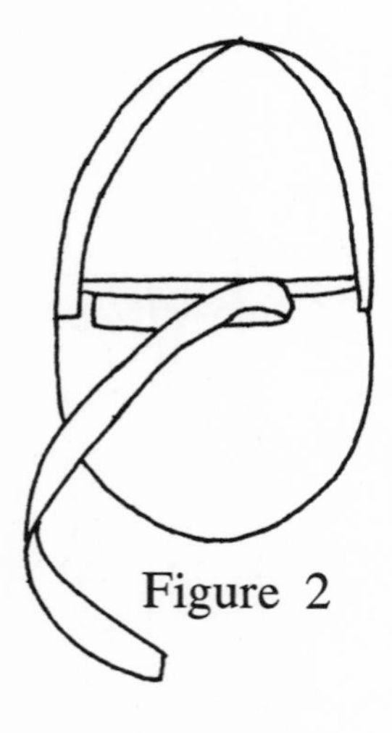
Figure 2

How to Make It:

1. Following Step 1 of the previous egg bell project, cut egg shell almost in half for basket.
2. Paint shell basket inside and out any desired color. Let dry, then spray or brush on 2 coats of fixative.
3. Cut a 5- or 6-inch piece of ribbon. Glue one end of ribbon to one side of basket and the other end to the other side to make a handle (Fig. 1).
4. Brush a thin line of glue around top edge of basket. Carefully stick ribbon on glue line (Fig. 2). Be sure to cover ends of ribbon handle. Make a tiny ribbon bow and glue it on ribbon band, hiding the place where the two ends meet (Fig. 3). Fill basket with tiny artificial flowers if desired.

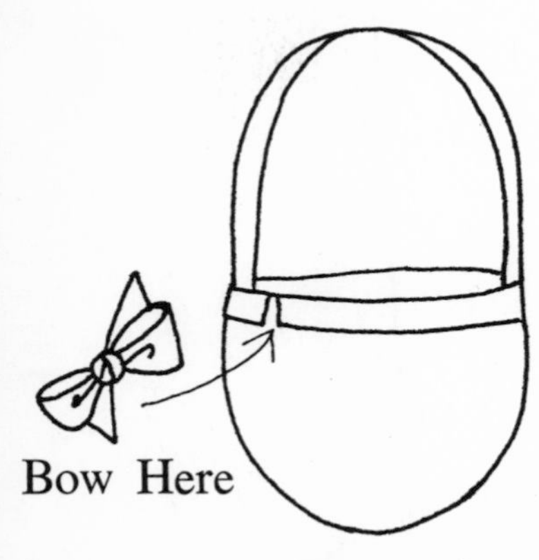

Figure 3

Print an Egg

Adding simple designs to a plain egg is easy when you print them. With the help of a pencil eraser, a sponge, even a potato, a plain egg graduates from being just a pretty colored egg into the class of decorated egg.

Ever since eggs were first colored, people have been devising methods for putting designs on eggs. And since not all eggers felt talented enough to hand-paint designs with a brush, they experimented and developed methods of printing.

Many different printing props have been used to make designs. Chances are that if you look in drawers or in places where odds and ends of no particular value collect in your home, you will find objects that would make a print. An embossed design on the cap of a felt marking pen, a birthday candleholder, a fancy button, an interesting bottlecap may be some of the things you will find that you could experiment with.

Begin your printing with the methods explained in this chapter. Then go on and see if you can't develop a basketful of eggs using other found printing props.

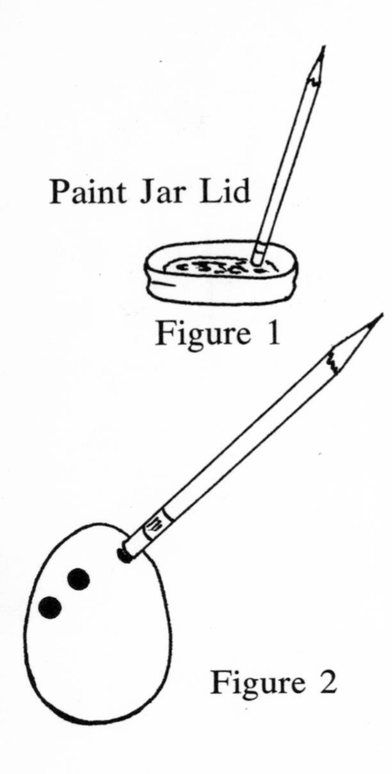

Figure 1

Figure 2

Printed Polka Dots

You Will Need:
plain eggs, any color
paints
pencils with new erasers
fixative
damp sponge
fine-point paintbrush or felt marker

How to Make It:
1. Select a color of paint lighter or darker than your plain egg. Gently shake jar of paint and carefully remove lid. To print a polka dot, use the paint that remains in the lid. Dip pencil eraser flat down in the paint (Fig. 1), then stamp it on the egg surface (Fig. 2). (Make a few practice dots on paper first to get acquainted with this technique.) Print polka dots all over one half of the egg, let paint dry, then print the other half. When egg is thoroughly dry, seal it with fixative. And remember to clean the lid before replacing it on the jar.
2. Print several eggs, arranging dots in assorted designs like those shown or using your own ideas. Make dots in a variety of colors. (Always wipe eraser with a damp sponge when going from one

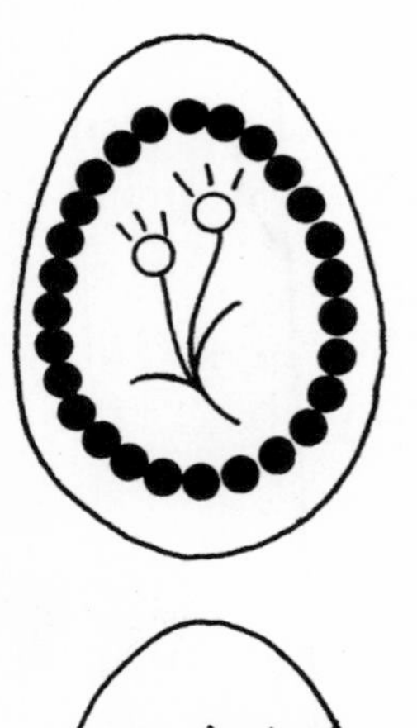

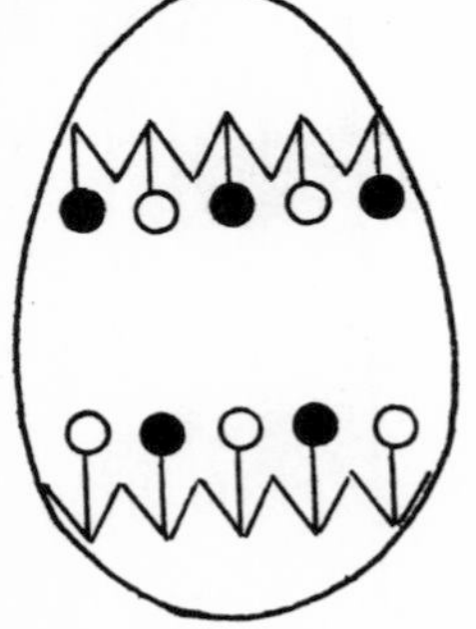

color to another.) Use a fine-point paint-brush or felt marker to add details like stems and leaves.

Pencil Eraser Designs

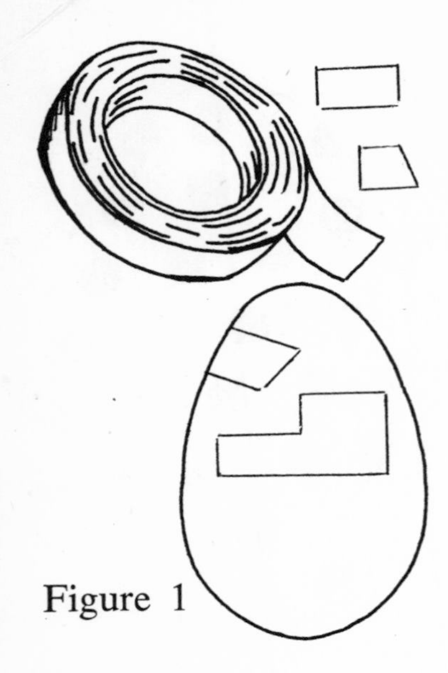
Figure 1

Op Art

You Will Need:
plain egg, any color
masking tape
paints
paintbrush or sponge
fixative
scissors
pencil with new eraser

How to Make It:
1. Spray or brush egg with a light coat of fixative. (This will protect painted surface from possibly being pulled away later by masking tape.)
2. Cut strips, squares, and rectangles from masking tape. Apply tape shapes here and there on egg in any arrangement you wish (Fig. 1). Do not cover egg completely with tape; let lots of the plain egg color show.
3. Using a lighter or darker color than used for the plain egg, paint or sponge areas of egg not covered by the masking-tape shapes. When paint is thoroughly dry, remove tape pieces.
4. Using a new pencil eraser, stamp dots here and there on the egg using a different color paint. When dry, finish with 2 coats of fixative.

Print a Petal

You Will Need:
plain egg, any color
cotton swabs (such as Q-Tips)
paints
fixative

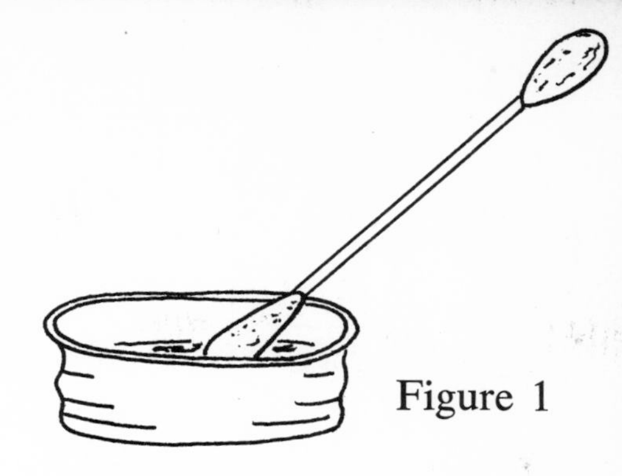
Figure 1

How to Make It:
1. Shake paint jar gently. Remove lid carefully. Use paint remaining in lid for printing.
2. Twist a cotton swab between your fingers to be sure cotton is smooth and tight on the stick. Roll one end of the swab in paint until cotton is evenly saturated but not dripping with paint (Fig. 1).

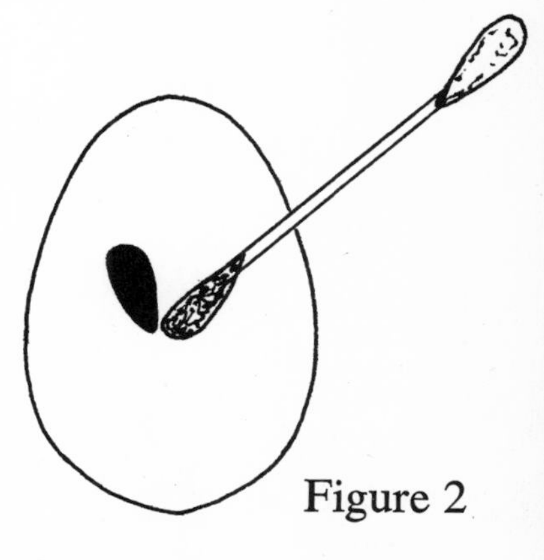
Figure 2

3. Petal shape is made by touching side of swab to the egg surface. Make a few practice prints on paper first so that you will know how much pressure to apply in order to obtain a good petal print. Now print the petal shape on the egg (Fig. 2). Experiment with the shape to make a variety of designs. Several petals put together in a circle will make a flower. One shape alone can be a leaf. For dots, print with the end of the cotton swab. Be sure to use a separate swab for each color of paint.
4. When printed eggs are dry, finish them with a fixative.

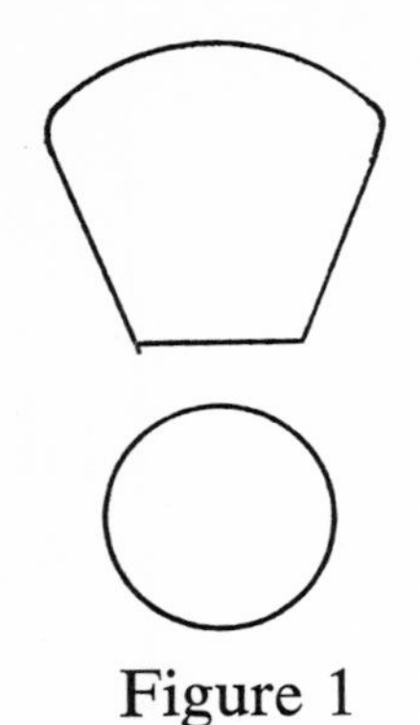

Figure 1

Sponge a Flower

You Will Need:

plain egg painted white
paint in 3 bright compatible colors, such as orange, pink, and bright yellow; or turquoise, lime, and purple
synthetic sponge about ½ inch thick (different sponge textures will give different effects)
scissors
fixative

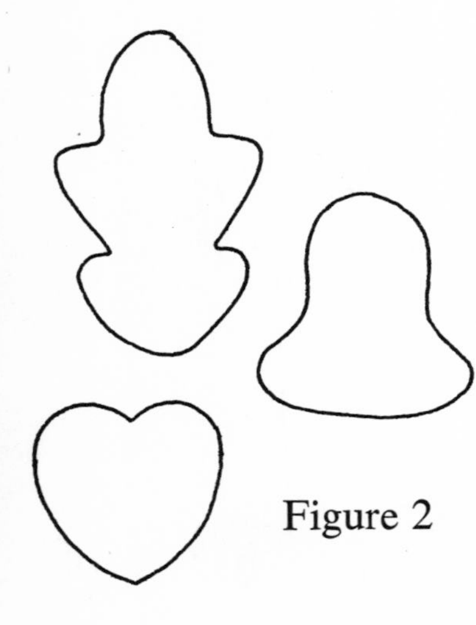

Figure 2

How to Make It:

1. From the sponge, cut a circle and a petal shape like those shown in Figure 1. (You can cut them freehand or make paper patterns from Fig. 1.) Or cut other simple shapes like the leaf, bell and heart shown in Figure 2.

2. Shake jars of paint gently and remove lids carefully. Use paint remaining in lid for printing. Rinse cutout sponge pieces in clean water and remove excess moisture by squeezing in paper towels. Sponge should be barely damp. Dip sponge circle in yellow paint. Stamp circle on egg. Dip sponge petal in pink paint, stamp petals around edge of yellow circle (Fig. 3). (Dip sponge in paint occasionally as you work to ensure a good print.) Stamp

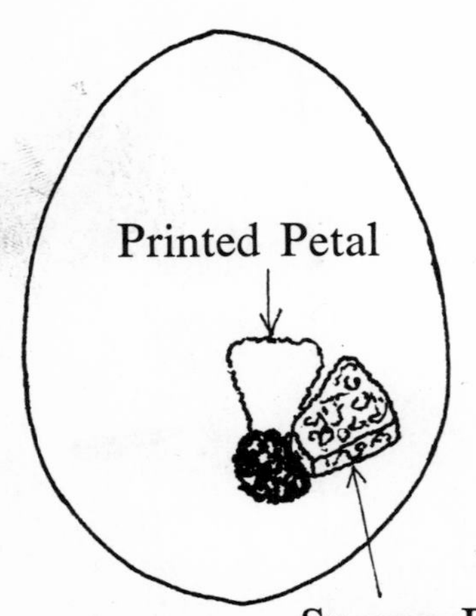

Figure 3

the yellow circle again right on top of the first printed circle.

3. Wash sponge shapes thoroughly and remove excess moisture. Dip circle in orange paint and stamp on egg. Print yellow petals around circle. (Petals of this flower can slightly overlap petals of the first flower.)

4. Continue printing flowers until egg is covered. Make orange flowers with yellow centers, pink flowers with orange centers, and yellow flowers with pink centers. Be sure to wash sponge shapes every time you change paint colors.

5. Finish egg with 2 coats of fixative when paint is thoroughly dry.

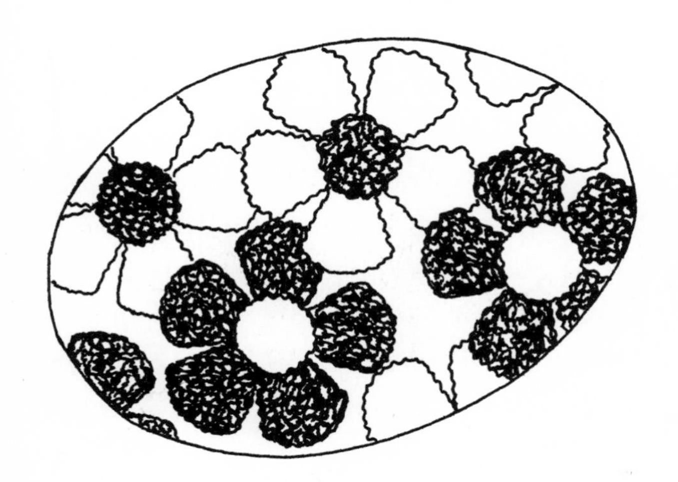

Print With a Potato

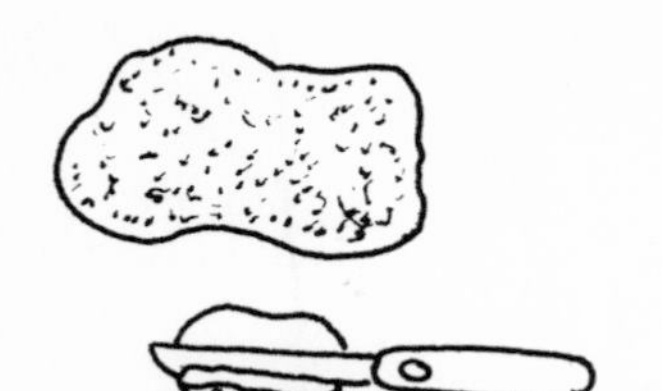

Figure 1

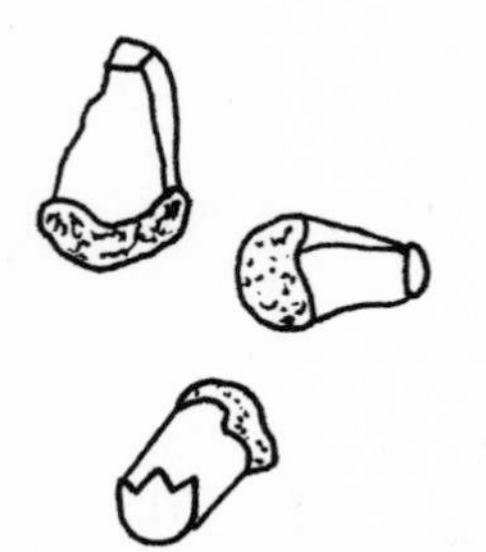

Figure 2

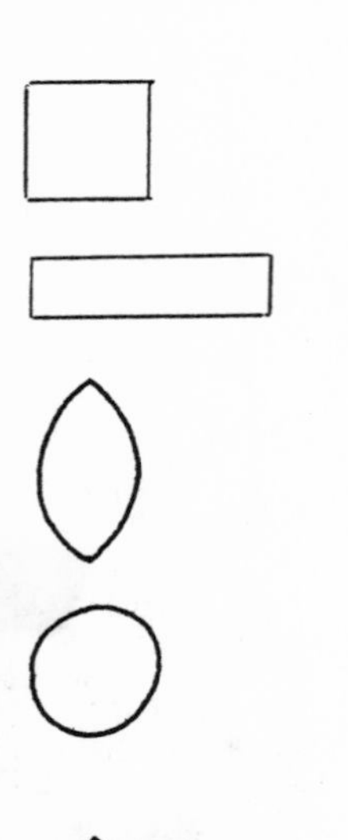

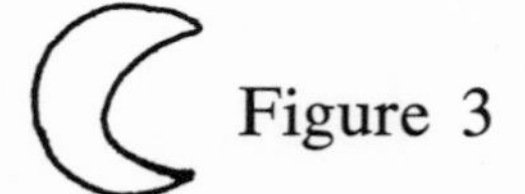

Figure 3

You Will Need:
plain egg, any color
small, firm potato
paring knife
paints
paintbrush, ½ inch wide
paper towels
fixative

How to Make It:
1. With the paring knife, cut potato into several small pieces (Fig. 1). (Ask an adult to help you with this step.) Using knife, trim the raw end of one piece into a shape. This could be a square, circle, triangle, or oval (Fig. 2). (Do not trim or carve the skin end of the potato. This is the end you will hold in your hand when you print.) Take another potato piece and trim it into a different shape. Repeat with all the potato pieces, making each one a different shape such as those shown in Figure 3. The completed potato pieces will be your printing stamps.
2. Gently blot ends of the potato stamps with absorbent paper towels to remove excess water in the potato. (The surface of each stamp should be dry.)

3. Using a paintbrush, apply an even layer of paint to one of your potato stamps (Fig. 4). Print stamp on egg (Fig. 5). Press the stamp straight down, then lift it straight up.

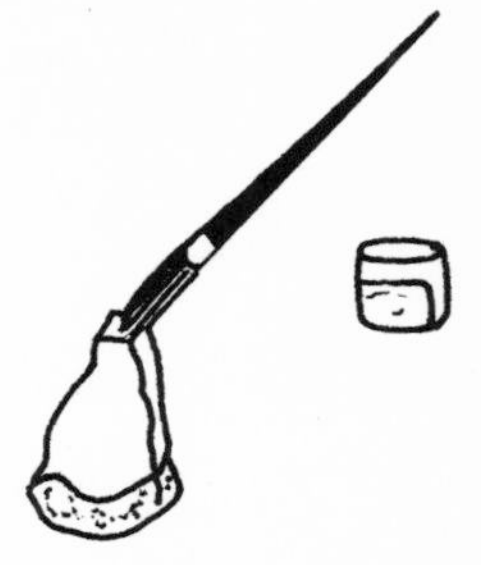

Figure 4

4. Use your stamps to print a variety of designs on eggs.

Do all your printing in one day because the potato will eventually shrink and dry up and so will have to be discarded. New stamps will have to be made for your next printing session. Always remember to remove one color of paint with a wet paper towel before changing to a different color.

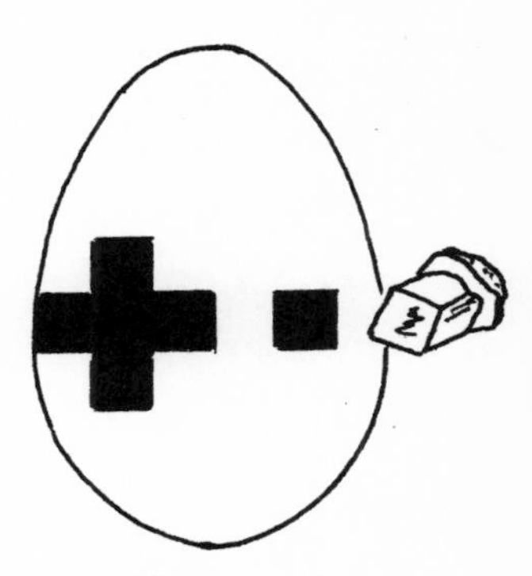

Figure 5

Potato printing is a simple method developed by the Pennsylvania Dutch to use on fabric and paper as well as on eggs. All sorts of designs can be carved into the potato, such as simple faces, hearts, letters, and animal shapes. Designs can be made large or small, so long as they fit the egg you plan to use.

6. Spray or brush completed egg with a fixative.

Paint an Egg

Hand-painted eggs allow you to be really creative. Some of the loveliest eggs are those with hand-painted scenes, or with icons or other religious symbols, all-over motifs of flowers, or geometric designs.

When you create hand-painted eggs, you can sketch a design lightly on the egg with pencil, or work freehand, or transfer a design. (Embroidery designs and transfers are good sources for ideas.) You can paint any design or picture you want on an egg, or make it to fit a special occasion—a snowman on a Christmas egg, a bunny on an Easter egg, a mortarboard hat and diploma on an egg for a graduation, a pair of booties, a name and birthdate on an egg to celebrate the arrival of a new baby.

The designs in this chapter are only suggestions to get you started on your own hand-painted creations. You'll be surprised what you can do when you pick up a brush, dip it in paint, and go artistic on an egg.

Paisley

You Will Need:
plain egg, any color
tracing and carbon paper
piece of stiff paper
pencil
scissors
paints and brushes
fixative

How to Make It:
1. Trace the paisley designs and transfer them to the paper with carbon. Cut out all three paisley patterns.
2. Lay paisley patterns on the egg one at a time and trace around them lightly with pencil. Cover the egg with the paisley designs arranged in a pleasing pattern, but don't crowd or overlap any of the shapes.
3. Paint each paisley a solid color. Let dry. Using a fine-point paintbrush, paint flower and circle details on each paisley. The tiny circles can be printed with the end of the paintbrush handle exactly as you used an eraser when you printed polka dots. Outline each paisley in black. Let dry, then spray or brush on fixative.

Paisley Designs

Red, White, and Blue

You Will Need:

plain egg, unpainted
red, white, bright blue, and bright yellow paints
paintbrushes
black fine-line felt marker
wide rubber band
pencil
fixative

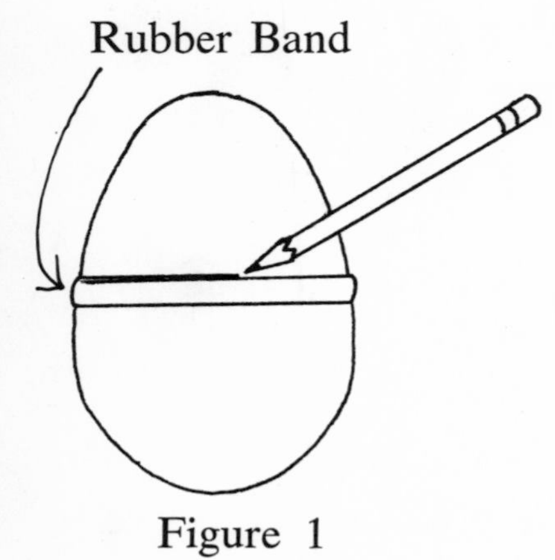

Figure 1

How to Make It:

1. Place rubber band crosswise around center of the egg. Using the rubber band as a guide, draw a line around the egg, dividing it exactly in half (Fig. 1). Remove rubber band.
2. With pencil, lightly draw vertical stripes around the bottom half of the egg (Fig. 2). There should be an even number made to fit the contour of the egg with all stripes meeting in the center at the bottom of the egg. (The rubber band can help you draw the stripes.)
3. Paint the bottom half of the egg alternate stripes of red and white. Let dry. Paint the top half of the egg bright blue. Let dry.
4. Following Figure 3, steps 1 through 4, sketch stars lightly with pencil all

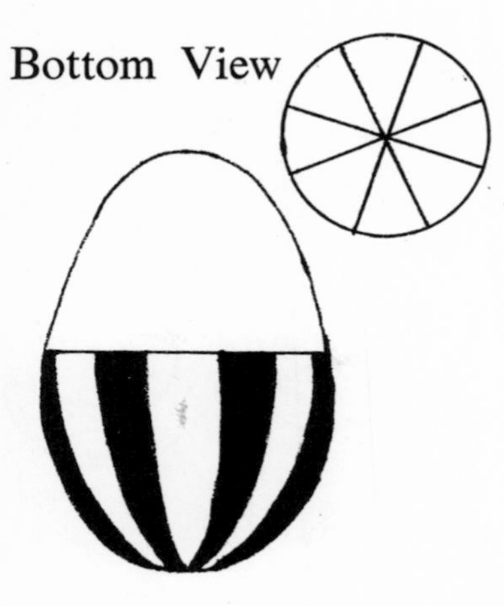

Figure 2

over top half of the egg. Paint stars bright yellow.

5. When paint is thoroughly dry, outline stars and stripes with black fine-line felt marker.

6. Spray or brush on 2 coats of fixative.

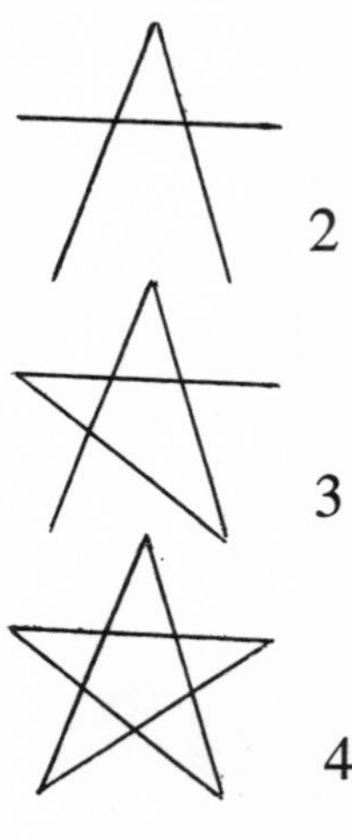

Figure 3

Peasant Style

You Will Need:

plain egg painted black

pastel or bright-colored paints (bright blue, turquoise, pink, yellow, white, bright green)

paintbrushes

pencil (white or yellow)

black fine-line felt marker, or fine-point paintbrush and black paint

fixative

How to Make It:

1. Using illustrations of eggs shown, lightly sketch a similar flowered design all over the egg with pencil. (Don't use a pattern. Peasant eggs are done free-hand.)
2. Paint designs using bright or pastel colors. Use a fine-point paintbrush for small parts of the design.
3. When paint is dry, add details and outline design with black fine-line felt marker. Allow to dry thoroughly, then apply fixative.

Black-and-white Geometrics

You Will Need:
plain egg painted white
black fine-line felt marker
small ruler
wide rubber band
pencil
fixative

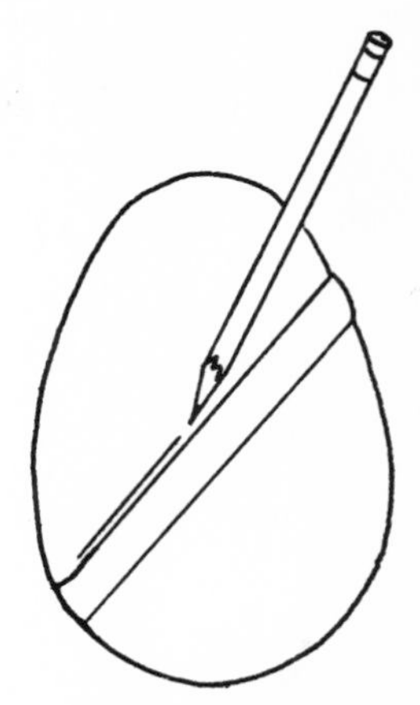
Figure 1

How to Make It:
1. With pencil and ruler sketch geometric design on egg. Put rubber band around egg to help draw diagonal lines and to divide egg in half and quarters (Fig. 1). Use rubber band for sketching long lines, ruler for short lines. Draw curved lines and circle freehand or trace around buttons or coins.
2. Paint parts of the design with the black marker. Completed egg will be a black-and-white geometric.
3. Finish with 2 coats of fixative.

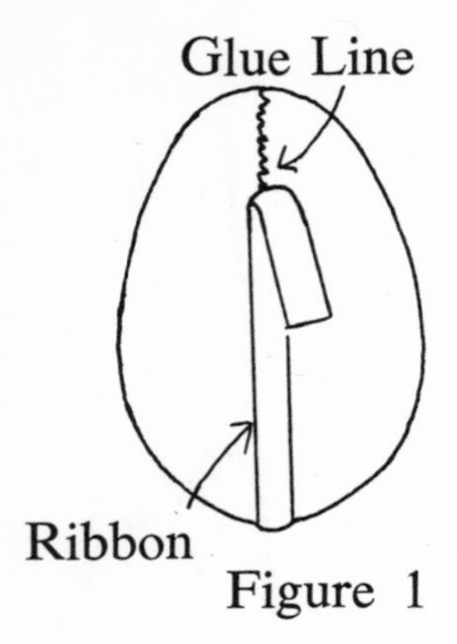

Figure 1

Design

Be My Valentine

You Will Need:

plain egg painted red or white (jumbo chicken or duck egg if possible)
tracing paper
pencil
paints and brushes
fixative
red or white narrow ribbon
glue and brush

How to Make It:

1. Trace design shown onto tracing paper. Transfer design to egg following directions on pages 29–30.
2. Paint design as desired. When thoroughly dry, spray or brush on 2 coats of fixative.
3. Using a brush, apply a thin line of glue around egg from top, down side, around bottom, and back up to the top. Neatly press ribbon on glue line (Fig. 1). Make a ribbon bow and glue it to top of egg.

Paint a Scene

You Will Need:

plain egg painted light blue (jumbo chicken or duck egg if possible)
tracing paper and pencil
paints, assorted colors including water-base metallic gold
fine-point paintbrushes
fixative

How to Make It:

1. Trace and transfer scenic design to egg. Lightly sketch a scalloped frame around design as shown in finished egg.
2. Paint design as desired. Let paint dry thoroughly, then paint scalloped frame metallic gold.
3. When dry, complete egg with 2 coats of fixative.

Scenic Design

People, Pets, and Things

When does an egg become more than just a plain or painted one? When it takes on character. This chapter of people, pets, and things is devoted to a storybook land of eggs. After you have made some of the characters like Humpty Dumpty and the Queen of Hearts, try creating others like the Three Kings for Christmas or a witch for Halloween. The bunny on page 69 might inspire you to make another animal, such as a little gray mouse. The number of creatures you can make is only limited by your imagination. So, put some character in your eggs.

Humpty Dumpty

You Will Need:

plain unpainted egg, the size of a chicken egg (for larger eggs, make larger patterns)
lid from cardboard egg carton
pencil
tracing and carbon paper
scissors
paints and paintbrush
glue and brush
fixative

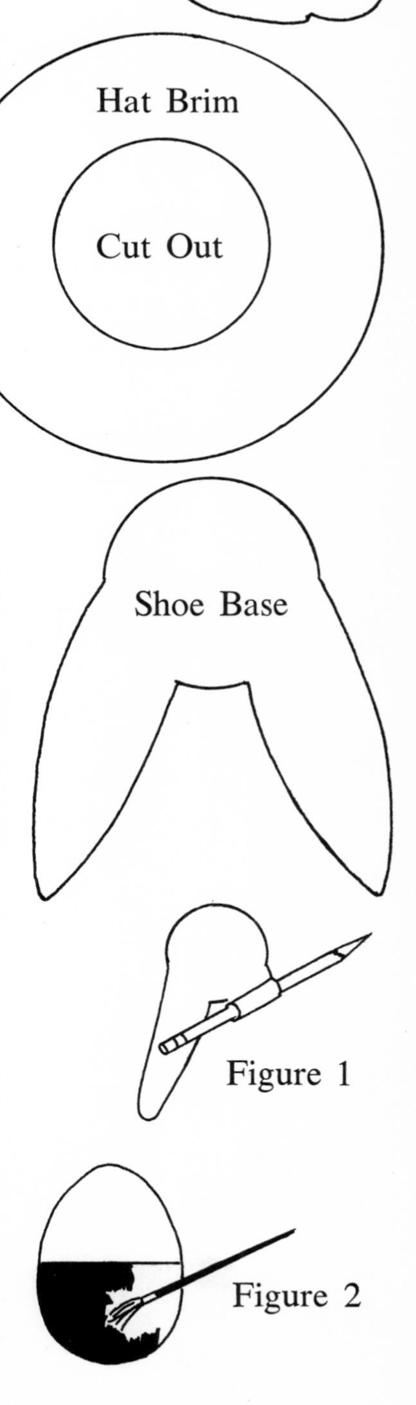

How to Make It:

1. Trace patterns for shoe base, arm and hat brim. Transfer to flat part of egg-carton lid and cut out. Be sure to transfer and cut out 2 arms. Soak shoe base in water (as described on page 29). When cardboard is pliable, curl toes of shoes around a pencil (Fig. 1). Set shoe base aside to dry.

2. Paint top half of the plain egg white. This will be Humpty Dumpty's head. Paint the bottom half (the broad end of the egg) bright blue (Fig. 2). Paint arms blue also, but make hands white. Paint hat brim and shoes green. (Egg-carton cardboard will require at least 2 coats of paint for good coverage.)

Figure 1

Figure 2

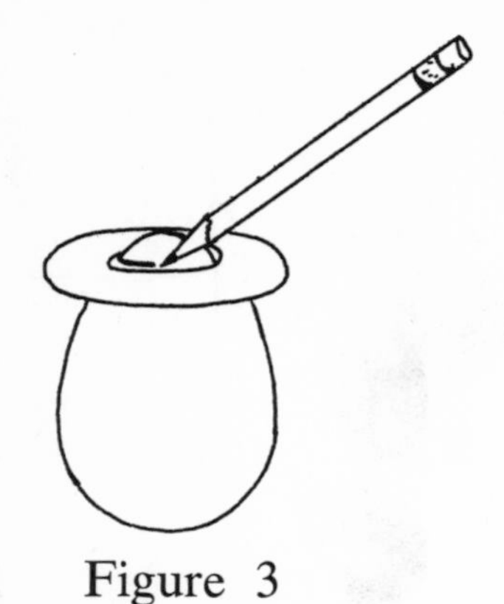

Figure 3

3. Set hat brim on top of Humpty Dumpty's head and lightly mark a circle where the hat will sit (Fig. 3). Remove brim. Below the marked circle, paint hair and face (Fig. 4). Above the penciled circle, paint the top of the egg green. This will be the hat crown. Let paint dry.

4. Now paint details like buttons, collar, and pockets on the body. Just make outlines with a fine-pointed paintbrush and black paint.

5. When paint is thoroughly dry, glue arms to sides of the egg body. Glue body on the shoe base. Finally, glue hat brim on head. Let glue dry and finish Humpty Dumpty with fixative.

Figure 4

Queen of Hearts

You Will Need:

plain unpainted egg, the size of a chicken egg
cardboard egg-carton lid
eggcup cut from cardboard egg carton
paints and brushes
tracing and carbon paper
pencil
scissors
glue and brush
fixative
sequins and beads (optional)

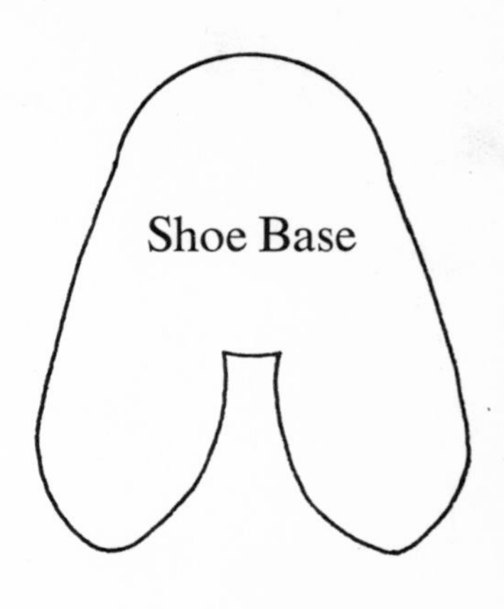

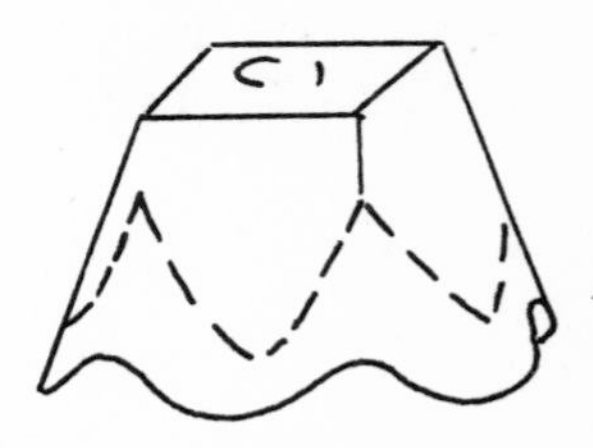

Figure 1

How to Make It:

1. Trace pattern for shoe base and arm. (See Humpty Dumpty and use same arm patterns.) Transfer to egg-carton lid and cut out 2 arms and 1 shoe base.
2. Draw a pointed petal shape on each side of the eggcup as shown in Figure 1. Cut cup on penciled lines. This will be the queen's crown (Fig. 2).

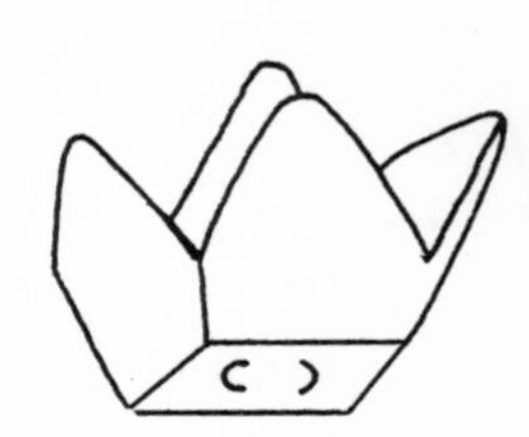

Figure 2

3. Paint top half (the narrow end) of egg and hands a skin color. Paint bottom half of egg and sleeves red. Paint shoe base black and paint crown metallic gold or yellow. Let paint dry.
4. Paint a white fuzzy collar around neck of egg and white cuffs at end of

each sleeve. When paint is dry, add black ermine markings to the collar and cuffs (Fig. 3).

5. Paint hair and facial features on top half of egg (Fig. 4).

6. Glue arms to sides of egg body. Glue egg on shoe base and crown on top of head. If desired, trim crown with sequins and beads. Spray or brush on fixative before adding beads.

Figure 3

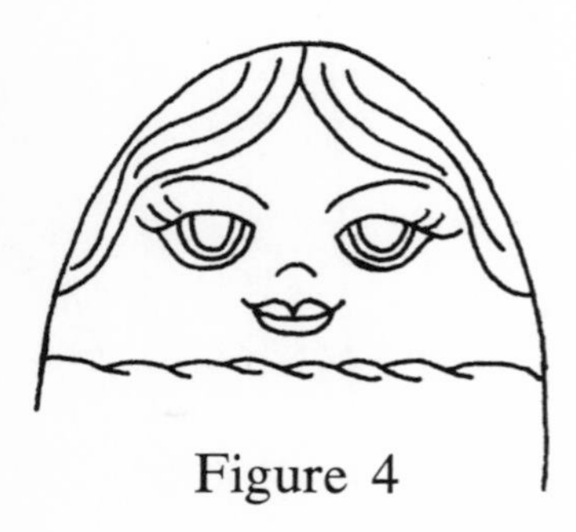

Figure 4

Clown

You Will Need:
plain unpainted egg, the size of a chicken egg
cardboard egg-carton lid
eggcup cut from cardboard egg carton
paints and brushes
pencil
tracing and carbon paper
scissors
glue
fixative
small feather (optional)

How to Make It:
1. Trace ear pattern and transfer to carton lid. Trace shoe base and sleeve from Humpty Dumpty, page 61, and transfer to lid. Cut out 2 sleeves, 2 ears, and 1 shoe base. Soak ears in water until pliable, then bend tabs back.
2. Cut eggcup so that it is about ¾ inch deep from top to bottom edge (Fig. 1). Then cut edge into irregular points (Fig. 2). This will be the clown's hat.
3. Paint ears and hands and top half of egg white. Paint bottom half of egg and sleeve purple. Make hat and shoe base yellow. Let dry, then paint a pointed yellow collar around neck and pointed

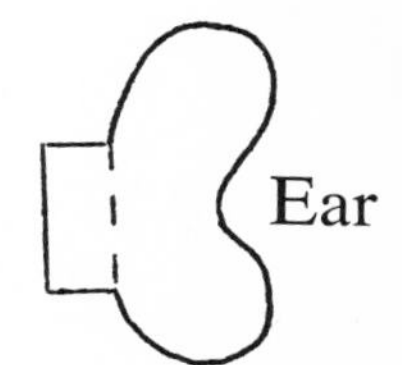

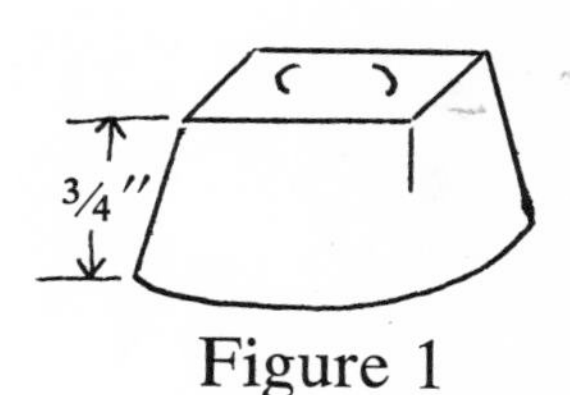

Figure 1

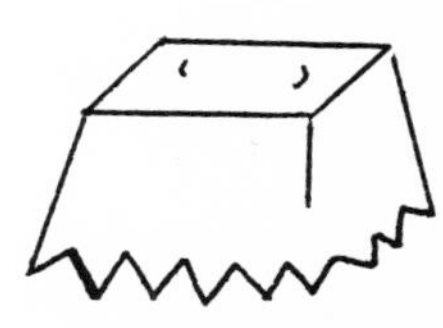
Figure 2

yellow cuffs at end of sleeves. Put a yellow pompon on the body (print it with a pencil eraser).

4. Paint facial features and hair on top half of egg. Make white polka dots all over body by dipping end of brush handle in paint in jar lid and stamping egg.

5. Glue an ear on each side of head. Glue sleeves in place, then stick egg to shoe base. Glue hat to top of head.

6. Spray or brush on 2 coats of fixative. When dry, glue feather to side of hat if desired.

Doll

You Will Need:
plain unpainted egg, the size of a chicken egg
cardboard egg-carton lid
carbon and tracing paper
pencil
scissors
paints and brushes
glue
fixative
narrow ribbon (pink, blue, or white)

Shoe Base

Bonnet

How to Make It:

1. Trace patterns for bonnet, shoe base, and arm (use Humpty Dumpty's arm), and transfer to egg-carton lid. Cut out one bonnet, shoe base, and 2 arms. Soak bonnet in water. When pliable, mold it over the small end of the egg so that it forms a nice curved shape (Fig. 1). Set bonnet aside to dry.
2. Paint top half (small end) of egg a skin color. Paint bottom quarter of egg white (Fig. 2). When dry, paint a pink dress on egg, starting at neck and ending just over the top of the white-painted bottom quarter. Paint sleeve pink and hands a skin color. Make shoe base and bonnet white. Let all pieces dry. Then

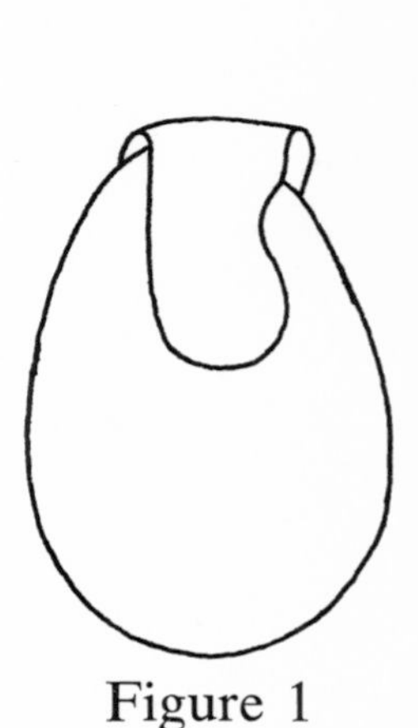

Figure 1

Skin Color

White

Figure 2

paint hair and facial features on top half of egg (Fig. 3).

3. Glue arms to side of egg body and bonnet over top of head. Glue body to shoe base. Let glue dry, then spray or brush on 2 coats of fixative. Make 3 tiny ribbon bows. Glue a bow to each side of the bonnet and one on front of body at neck.

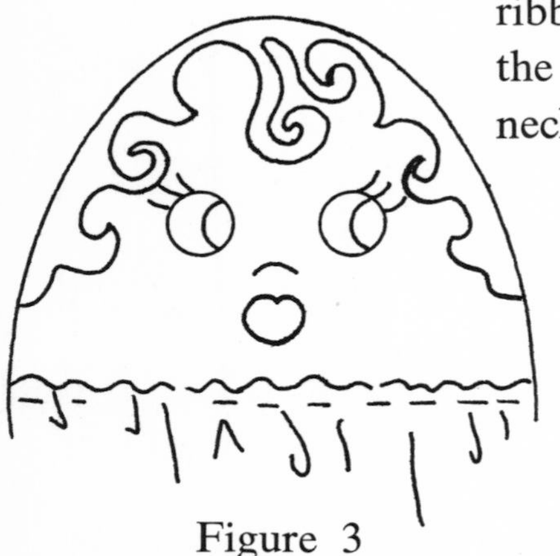

Figure 3

Bunny

You Will Need:
plain unpainted egg, chicken-egg size
cardboard egg-carton lid
2 roly-poly eyes
scissors
paints and brushes
tracing and carbon paper
glue
corsage pin
wooden matchstick and thread

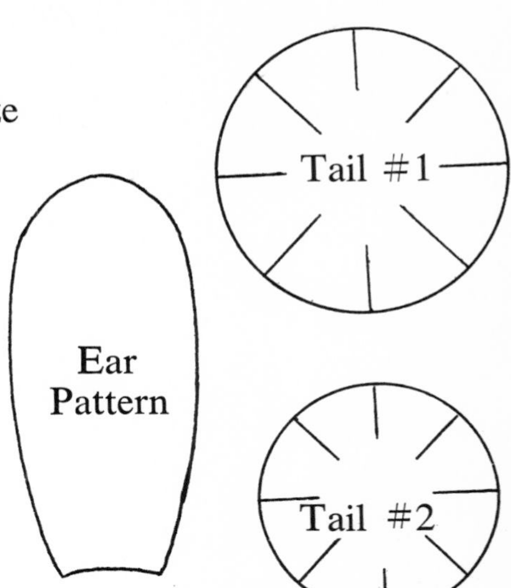

How to Make It:
1. Trace ear and tail patterns and transfer to lid of egg carton. Cut out 1 of each tail section and 2 ears. Soak all pieces in water until pliable. Shape ears so that they curve up slightly (Fig. 1), and so that the bottom of the ear fits flat against side of egg. With scissors, fringe edge of both tail sections as indicated on patterns. Bend up some of the fringed sections. Set ears and tail aside to dry.
2. Paint egg and ears purple and both tail sections white. When dry, paint a pink inner ear on each ear (Fig. 2). Glue roly-poly eyes on large end of egg, then paint on a nose, mouth, whiskers,

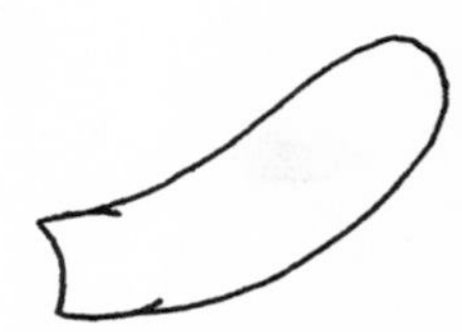
Figure 1

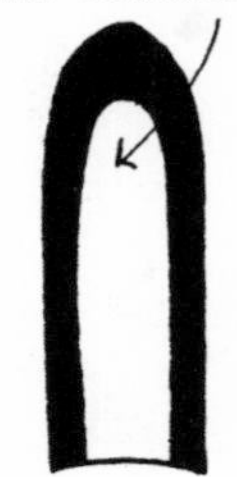

Figure 2

Figure 3

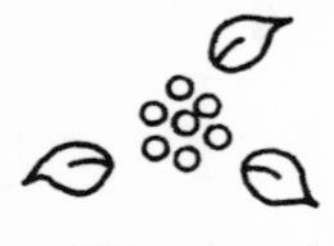
Figure 4

and eyelashes (Fig. 3). (If roly-poly eyes are unavailable, paint on eyes instead.)

3. When egg is thoroughly dry, paint flowers widely scattered all over the egg body. Put a little white and a little pink paint in separate jar lids. Use the end of your paintbrush handle to stamp dots that form a flower like the one shown in Figure 4. Make some flowers pink with white centers and others white with pink centers. When flowers are dry, paint on small green leaves if desired.

4. Glue an ear to each side of bunny's head. Glue the small tail on top of the large tail section, then glue the tail to the back of the bunny's body.

5. To hang bunny, carefully make a hole in the top center of the egg body. Enlarge hole enough to insert a threaded matchstick (see page 25, method 1).

6. Complete bunny with 2 coats of fixative. If you would rather have your bunny walk than fly, skip step 5 and glue a plastic curtain ring to the bunny's tummy.

Bird

You Will Need:

plain unpainted egg, the size of a chicken egg
cardboard egg-carton lid
tracing and carbon paper
pencil
scissors
paints and brushes
2 roly-poly eyes
glue
fixative
wooden matchstick and thread

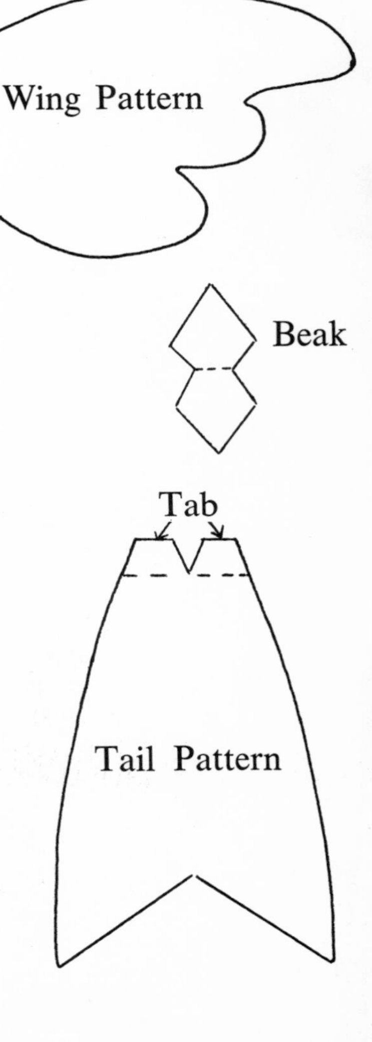

How to Make It:

1. Trace beak, tail, and wing patterns; transfer them to the egg-carton lid. Cut out one beak and tail and two wings. Soak beak and tab end of tail in water. When pliable, fold beak in half and bend tail tabs down. While cardboard is still damp, press tabs against large end of egg so they curve slightly and will later fit the contour of the egg.
2. Paint egg, wings, and tail blue, beak yellow. When paint is dry, glue the roly-poly eyes on the front end (small end) of the egg body, then paint on eyelashes.
3. Now put a design all over the egg. Use your own idea or paint flowers like

those on the bunny egg or make polka dots (see page 44). Let design dry.

4. Brush a line of glue along fold of beak and stick beak to front of egg. (You may have to hold it in place until it sticks by itself.) Put glue on tabs and stick tail to back of egg. Now glue a wing to each side of body. Put glue on front end of wing only.

5. To hang egg, see step 5 for Bunny Egg. Complete bird with two coats of fixative.

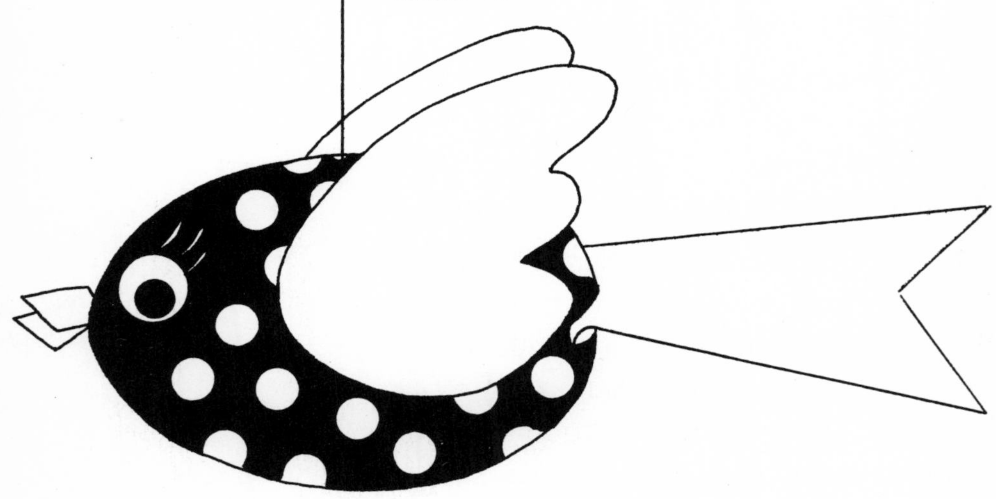

Fish

You Will Need:
plain egg painted orange
cardboard egg-carton lid
tracing and carbon paper
pencil
scissors
black paint and brush
2 roly-poly eyes
glue
fixative
wooden matchstick and thread
corsage pin

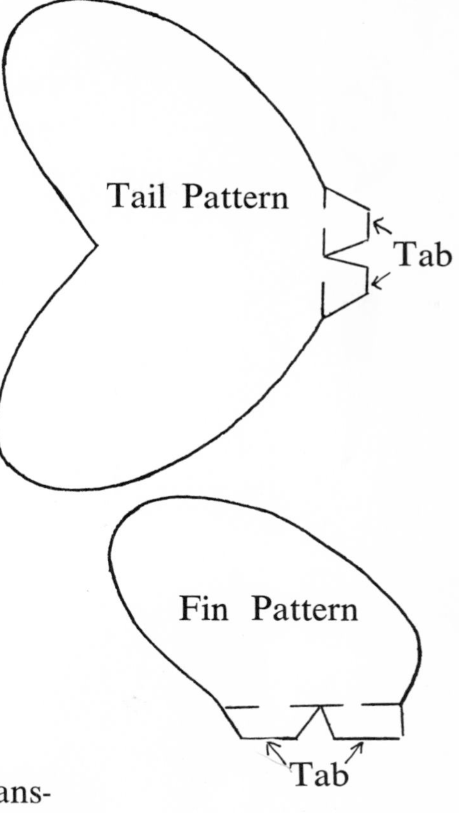

How to Make It:
1. Trace tail and fin pattern and transfer to egg-carton lid. Cut out one tail and 2 fins. Soak tab ends of all pieces in water until pliable. Take one fin and bend one tab in one direction and the other tab in the opposite direction (Fig. 1). Do the same thing with the other fin and the tail. Let all pieces dry.
2. Paint fins and tail black. Glue eyes on broad end of orange body. Then paint on a black mouth and add black eyelashes (Fig. 2). Now paint black tiger stripes on body. Let paint dry.
3. Glue tail to back end of body, then

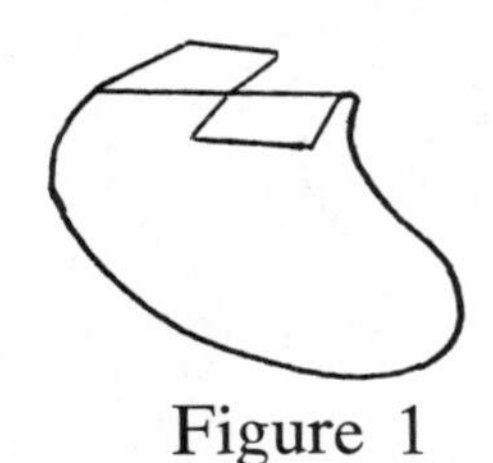
Figure 1

Figure 2

glue a fin to the top and the bottom of body.

4. To hang fish, make a hole in top of egg in front of fin with a corsage pin. Insert threaded matchstick (see page 25, method 1). Finish fish with 2 coats of fixative.

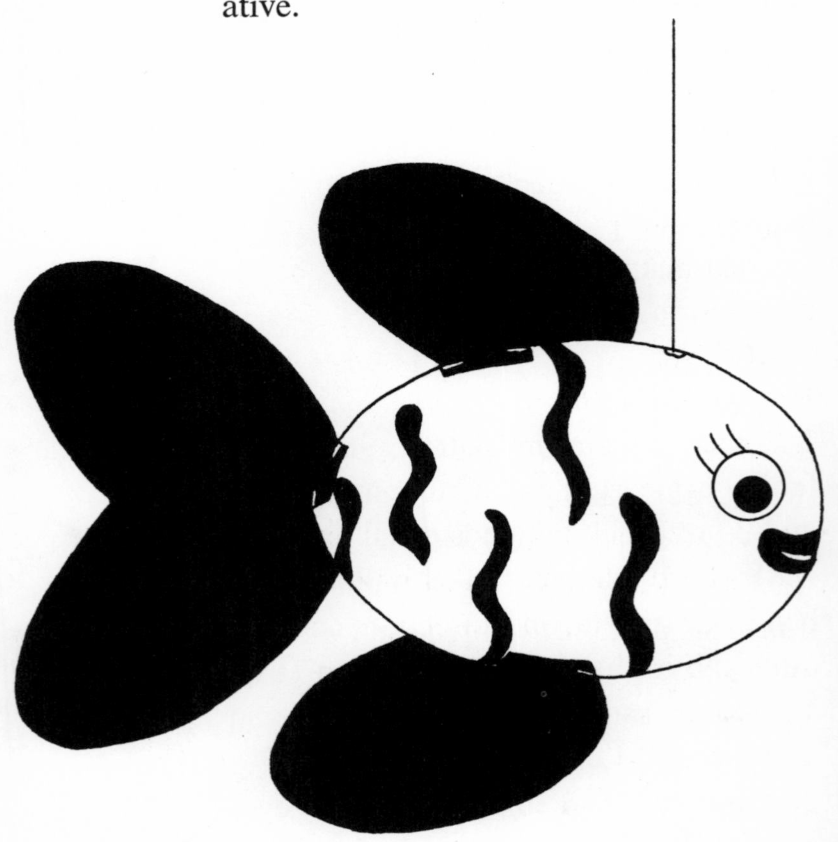

Egg Mobile

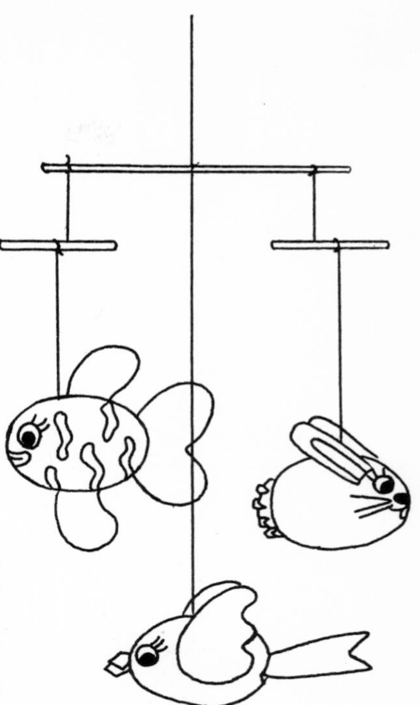

You Will Need:
Bunny, Bird, and Fish egg
one 9-inch and two 4-inch pieces of thin
dowel stick or coat-hanger wire
nylon fishing line or strong thread
scissors

How to Make It:
1. Following illustration, suspend fish and bunny from the 4-inch pieces of dowel stick. Then suspend these sticks from the ends of the 9-inch stick. Tie the bird in the middle of the long stick between the fish and the bunny. Put the bird on a long thread so it will hang lower than the other two eggs. You can also add a bug to your mobile. A bug is easy to make, using pipe-cleaner pieces for legs and thin flexible wire for antennae. Finally, tie a hanging thread to the center of the 9-inch stick and adjust all threads if needed to make a balanced mobile.

You can also make an interesting mobile using the following airplane egg project.

Airplane

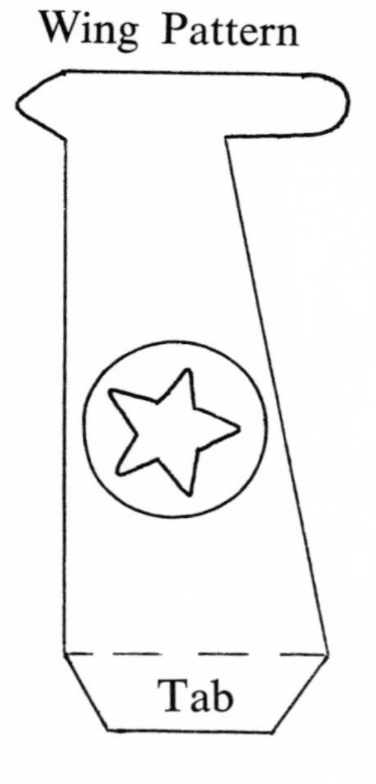

You Will Need:

plain egg painted red (extra-large or jumbo chicken egg)
cardboard egg-carton lid
tracing and carbon paper
pencil
scissors
red, white, and blue paint
paintbrushes
black fine-line felt marker
glue
fixative

How to Make It:

1. Trace wing and tail patterns and transfer to egg-carton lid. Cut out 2 wings and 1 tail. Soak tab ends of each piece until pliable. Bend wing tabs down; bend tail tabs down in opposite directions. While paper is still wet, mold tail tabs against end of egg so that they are slightly curved.
2. Paint tail and wings red and let dry. Paint a large white window around front end of egg and 3 small square windows on each side. When dry, outline windows with black marking pen. Paint insignia on wings, making circle blue and star white. When dry, outline with black pen.

3. Glue tail to back end of egg. Glue a wing to each side.
4. To hang, see Humpty Dumpty, page 61. Finish with 2 coats of fixative.

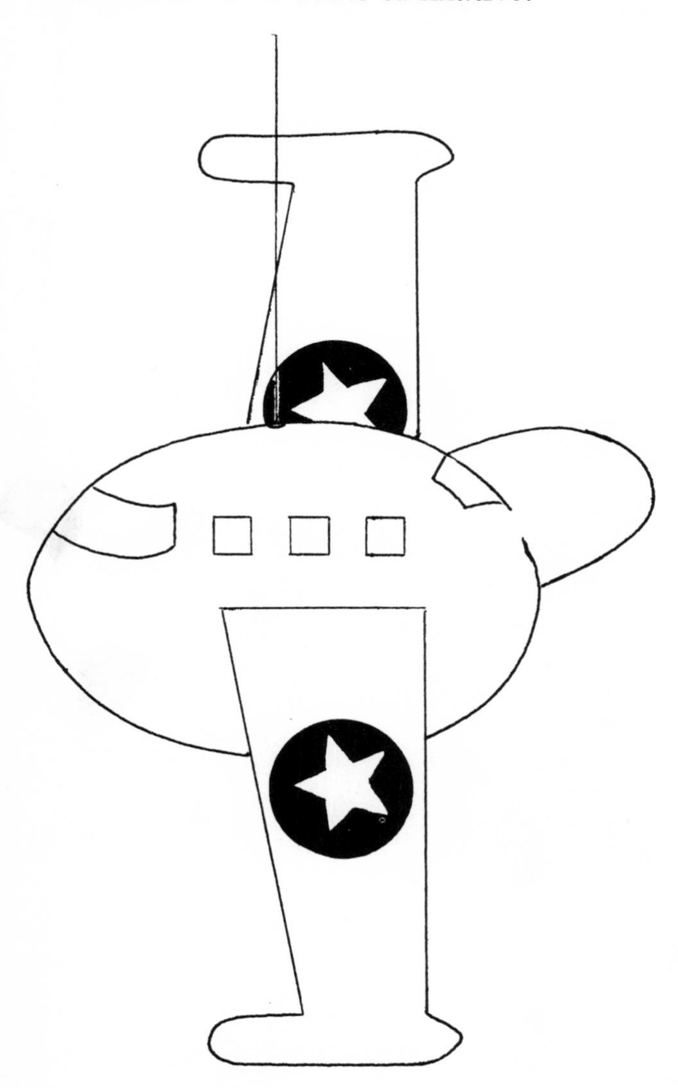

Egg House

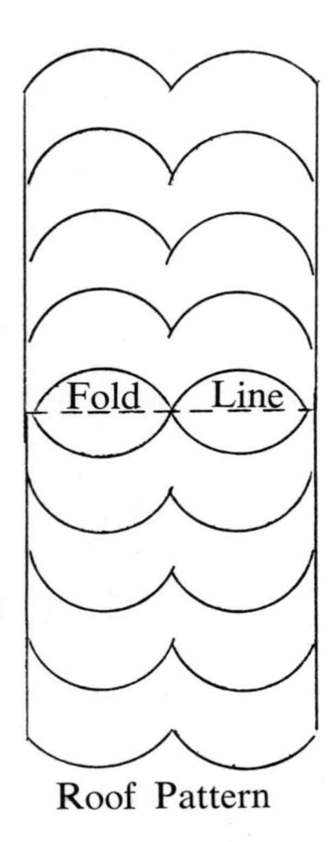

Roof Pattern

You Will Need:
plain egg painted light blue
cardboard egg-carton lid
paints and brushes
black fine-line felt marker
scissors
glue
fixative

How to Make It:
1. Trace patterns for roof and base sections, transfer them to egg-carton lid. Cut out 1 of each piece. Soak roof in water until pliable, then gently fold it in half on fold line. Set roof aside to dry.
2. Glue section 2 of base on top of section 1. Let glue dry.
3. Paint roof a bright color such as red or royal blue. When dry, use black marker to paint on shingle lines as shown

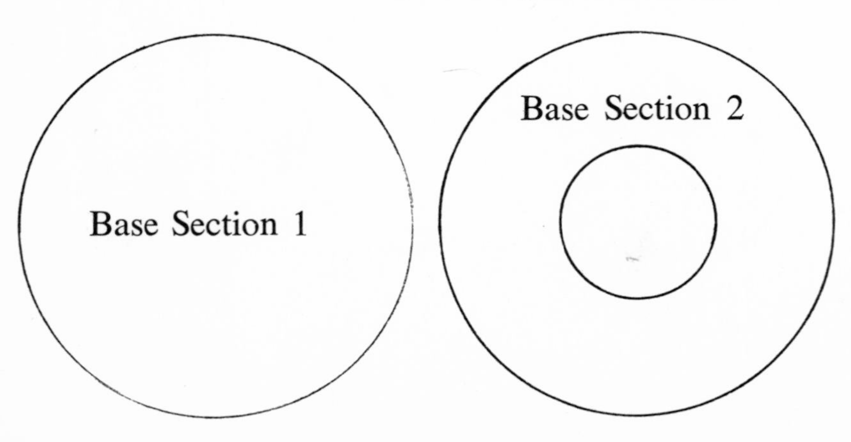

on pattern. Paint base green to represent grass.

4. When paint is thoroughly dry, set roof on top of egg (the narrow end). Note where egg and roof touch. Remove roof and apply glue to those spots only. Glue roof on top of egg, holding it in place until it sticks by itself (Fig. 1).

5. Paint doors and windows on the egg house (Fig. 2). Add a vine, bushes, and flowers (Fig. 3).

6. When paint is completely dry, glue egg to base. Apply a shallow puddle of glue in the cut-out section, then stand egg in glue. Let glue dry. Paint a dirt or stone walk on the base to represent a path to the front door. When dry, spray your egg house with fixative.

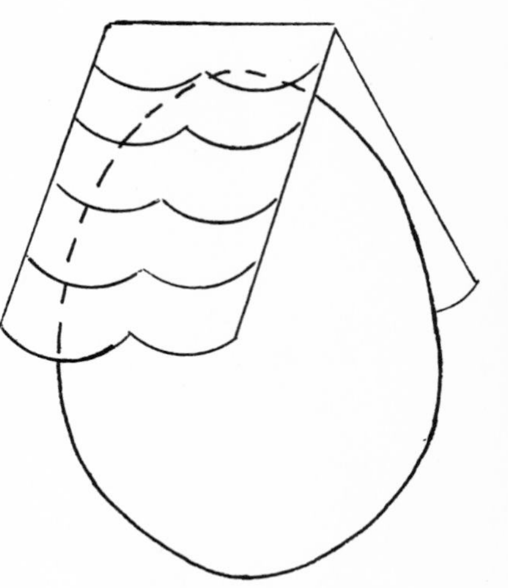

Figure 1

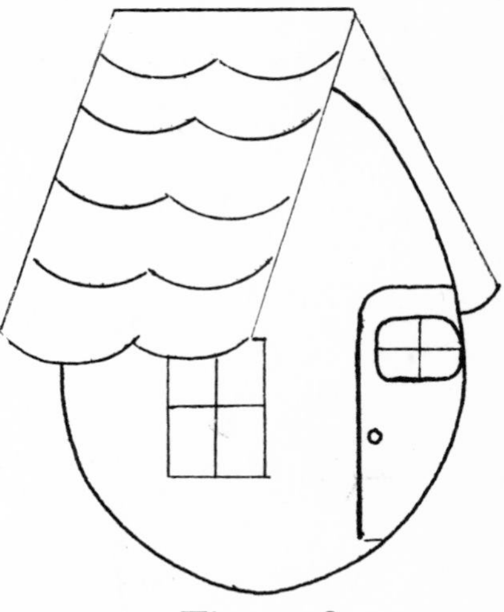

Figure 2

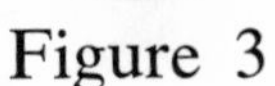

Figure 3

This little house is only one of many types you can make to build an egg village. You could also have a firehouse (use a goose egg if possible), a school, and even a diner. Use tall peaks and eggcups cut from an egg carton for different kinds of roofs, and oval-shaped bases for long egg buildings. Add miniature people, cars, and trees to make your village complete.

Church

House

Diner

Folk-art Eggs

In almost all countries around the world, egg decorating at Easter is a very old and extremely important tradition. Sometimes people in two different countries made eggs exactly the same but called them different names. Usually, however, people of one country decorated or painted their eggs in some way that made them different from eggs done by people in neighboring countries. When one country developed a style of decoration distinctively different from that of all other countries, the folk egg was born.

Most folk-art eggs carry a message or meaning of some sort or were created for a specific reason. Designs used were usually symbols inspired by nature or religion. A line or ribbon-like band painted continuously around an egg is a way of saying eternity; a ladder-like symbol suggests prayer; dots or small circles represent stars; deer mean wealth and prosperity; and flowers or leaves say life and growth. In the beginning all eggs were colored with homemade dyes extracted from natural products. For most egg decorating today, water and oil paints and commercial dyes have replaced homemade colors.

Decorated eggs were at first made only at Easter or for some other very special occasion. They were created for religious services and beliefs, to be given as gifts or used for decoration. Many became an all-important playing piece for traditional games such as egg rolling and egg knocking, while others played a definite role in a superstitious rite. Carrying a green egg on Maundy Thursday, for example, was thought to bring good luck. Egg decorating was so important and enjoyed by so many that in several countries it also became a Christmas tradition. In Poland, where many of the more popular Easter eggs were developed, people trim traditional Christmas trees with eggs decorated with paper and straw cutouts.

Pennsylvania Dutch Patchwork Eggs

You Will Need:
plain unpainted egg
assorted print and plain fabric scraps (firm cottons are best)
white glue or polymer medium
paintbrush, ½ inch wide
small damp sponge
scissors
spray fixative

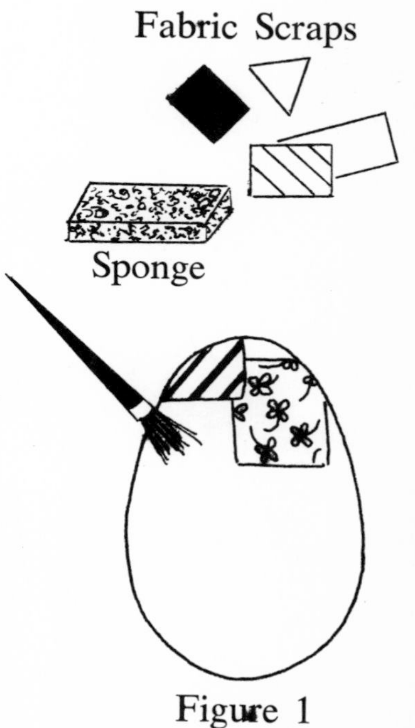

Figure 1

How to Make It:
1. Cut fabric scraps into small squares, rectangles, and triangles about ½ x ½ inch to 1 x 1 inch in size.
2. With the paintbrush, evenly spread a thin layer of glue or polymer medium over a small section of the egg shell. Immediately lay a fabric shape on top of the wet adhesive (Fig. 1). Press fabric tightly and smoothly against shell with the damp sponge. Brush another patch of adhesive right next to the first fabric shape and lay another fabric piece on top. The second fabric shape should slightly overlap the first. Repeat until the egg is covered with a layer of fabric

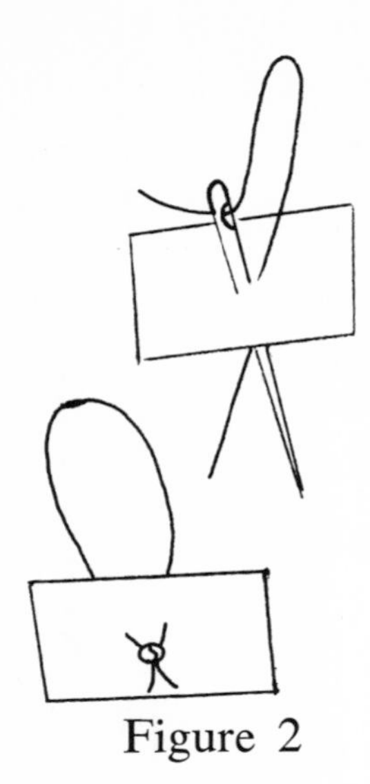

Figure 2

shapes like a patchwork quilt. Let egg dry thoroughly.

3. Brush complete egg with a coat of polymer medium. (Or use white glue thinned with water.) Let dry. Then spray with fixative if desired to keep egg clean.

4. If you wish to make a hanging egg, thread a needle with strong thread. Sew a hanging loop in the center of the first fabric shape, following Figure 2. Glue this shape to the top of the egg (Fig. 3), then continue covering egg as directed in Step 2.

Figure 3

Pennsylvania Dutch Scratch-carved Eggs

You Will Need:
fresh white eggs
onion skins (enough to fill a medium-size plastic bag)
small enamel pot
strainer
clean bowl
paper towels
pencil
sgraffito tool or a similar pointed tool

How to Make It:

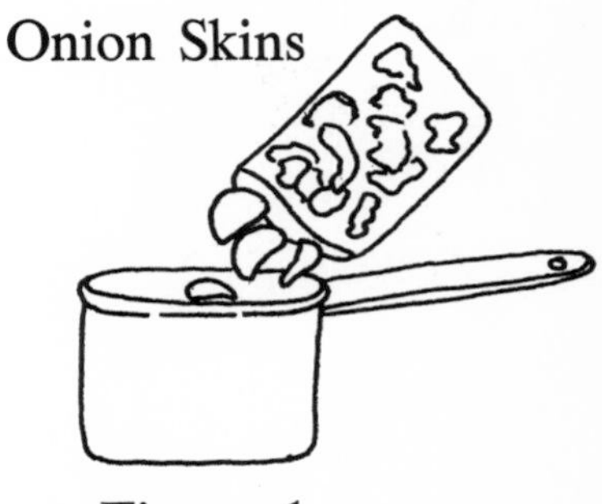

Figure 1

Figure 2

1. Put onion skins in the enamel pot (Fig. 1) and cover them with water until pot is about ¾ full. Put pot on stove and bring water to a boil. (Ask an adult to help you with this step.) Turn down heat to low and let water simmer (not boil) about an hour or until it becomes a deep brown or rich red color. Some skins produce red or maroon shades, while others give brown and reddish-brown shades. Remove dye from heat and allow it to cool. When cool, pour dye through a strainer and into a bowl to remove skins (Fig. 2). Discard skins and return dye to pot.

2. Place several fresh eggs in the dye bath. Do not try to dye too many eggs at one time. All eggs should be submerged in the dye without crowding.

3. Place the pot on the stove and bring dye to a boil. Turn down heat to a simmer and hard-cook the eggs about 30 minutes or until eggs are dyed a deep rich color and contents are thoroughly cooked. Occasionally turn eggs with a spoon while they are simmering to ensure an even coat of color. Remove pot from stove, then remove eggs from dye. Put eggs in a bowl of cool water until cool enough to handle. Set eggs on paper towel to dry until cold (Fig. 3). It is sometimes possible to use the same dye bath to color more eggs if all the coloring was not removed by the first eggs. Remember to let the dye cool before using again, then begin with Step 3. If your next batch of eggs does not come out a deep rich color, do not use them for the scratch-carved technique; instead, eat them or put them in an Easter basket. Eggs dyed with onion skins are perfectly safe to eat.

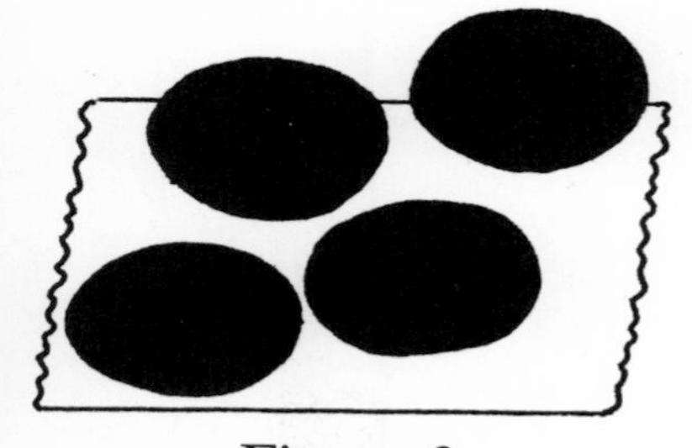

Figure 3

4. When eggs are cold they are ready to be scratch-carved. This term "scratch carving" is also known to artists and craftsmen as "sgraffito." It is the method of making designs by carefully scratch-

Figure 4

ing away color or paint to reveal the white undersurface (Fig. 4). With these dyed eggs you will remove the color by gently scratching away the onion-skin coloring, allowing the white egg surface to show (Fig. 5). Your final egg will be red or brown with a fine-line white design.

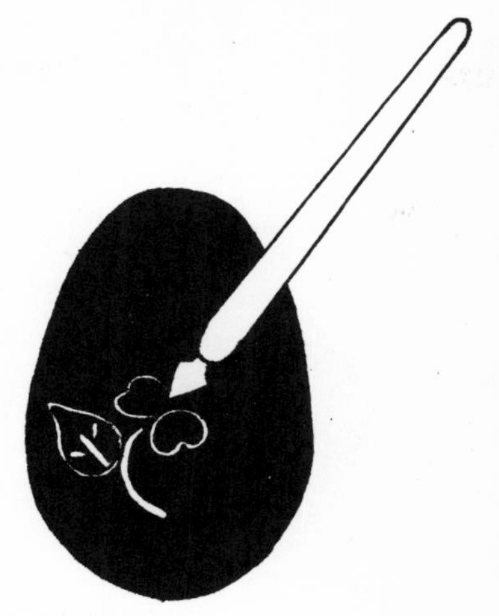

Figure 5

5. With pencil, lightly draw a simple design on a dyed egg. Keep in mind that flowers and designs for these eggs are in the Pennsylvania Dutch style. (Your local library may have books showing Pennsylvania Dutch designs.) Be sure to include the year and your name or the name of the person you are making the egg for. This was traditional with early scratch-carved eggs. You could also include a proverb or a Bible verse.

6. With a sgraffito tool or another pointed tool such as a nail, gently go over your penciled design. Carefully scratch the dyed surface, then scratch again until the white undersurface shows through. Do not try to remove the coloring with one scratch, but instead work as though you were working through several layers. Scratch all outlines first, then scratch away small areas within the outlines. When finished, you can spray your egg with a fixative to give it a nice rich shine.

English Pace Eggs

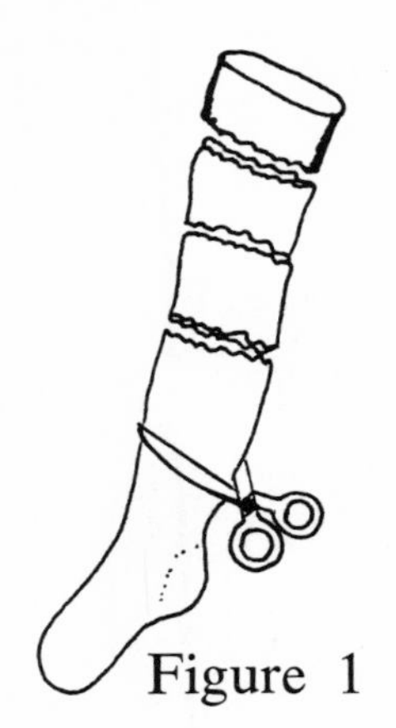
Figure 1

Figure 2

Figure 3

You Will Need:
fresh white eggs
assortment of natural products such as small leaves and flat flowers (violets, buttercups, phlox)
onion-skin dye (see Pennsylvania Dutch Scratch-carved Eggs)
clean nylon stockings (those which are no longer serviceable)
string
scissors
large bowl or pot of cool water
fixative

How to Make It:
1. Cut a stocking crosswise into tube-like sections about 5 inches long or 1 or 2 inches longer than the eggs you are using (Fig. 1). (Discard double-knit top and foot pieces.)
2. Select a fresh flower and some leaves. Lay them face down, flat against an egg (Fig. 2). Holding them in place with your fingers, insert egg in a stocking tube. Gather both ends of the stocking tightly together so that stocking is pulled tight and smooth around egg, holding the plant material securely in place. Tie stocking ends tightly with string (Fig.

3). If you need an extra hand for this step, ask a friend or an adult to help you. When you have several eggs tied and ready, place them in the pot of cooled onion-skin dye. Do not put too many eggs in the pot. The number of eggs you can dye at one time will depend on the amount of dye and the size of the pot.

3. Put pot on the stove and bring dye to a boil. Lower heat and gently simmer eggs about 20 to 30 minutes.

4. Remove pot from stove, then remove eggs from dye with a slotted spoon and place them in a bowl of cool water. When cool enough to handle, remove eggs from water and carefully take them from their stocking wrapper. The background of the eggs should be colored a shade of brown or red, and the imprint of the plant material should be white or a pastel color. When eggs are completely cold they can be sprayed with a fixative.

English Pace eggs were often used in games such as egg rolling and egg knocking.

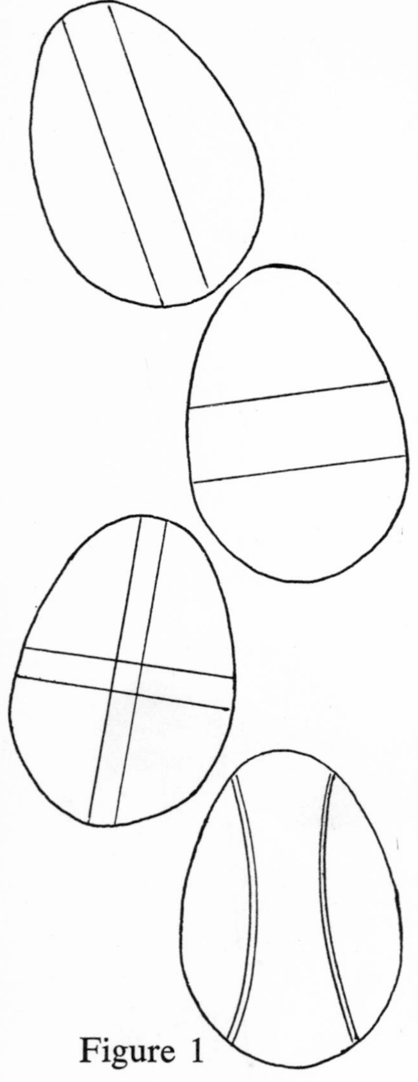
Figure 1

Czechoslovakian Eggs

You Will Need:

plain eggs painted rich, deep colors such as black, dark green, dark red, brown
paints and fine-point paintbrush
black fine-line felt marker, or pen and India ink
wide rubber band
pencil (use white or yellow for black or brown eggs)
fixative

How to Make It:

1. Designs for Czechoslovakian, Ukrainian, and Polish eggs are without number. Although each of those countries uses a different method of decorating eggs, all of them use the same symbols and designs. Some of the completed designs are simple; some are extremely intricate and require a great deal of patience. Almost all of the designs include a wide band or ribbon either lengthwise or crosswise around the egg. This band represents eternal or continuous life. Use

Little Baskets
Holy Trinity

Ribbon, Belt, or Band—
Endless Line of Eternity

the wide rubber band and a pencil to divide your egg into sections and to draw the eternal band. This band can be drawn on your egg in any one of the ways shown in Figure 1. The rubber band will also help you draw the triangles, rectangles, and many short lines that are also found in these folk designs.

2. Figure 2 illustrates some of the many symbols used in this type of folk egg. Use some of these symbols in the design for your egg. Lightly sketch your chosen design on the egg. Your first egg does not have to be intricate; keep the design simple.

3. Using a very fine paintbrush, paint the design with care and patience. Fine straight lines and outlines are done with the felt marker or with pen and India ink. Don't expect your first egg to be perfect, but do expect each egg you do to become better. Children of Slavic

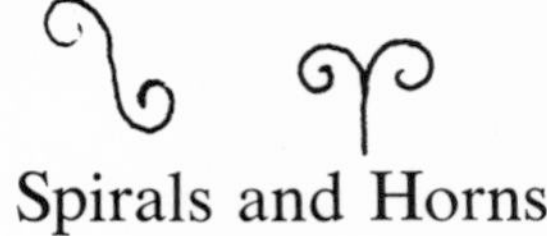

Spirals and Horns

Birds—Fertility

Grape Vine — Good Fruits

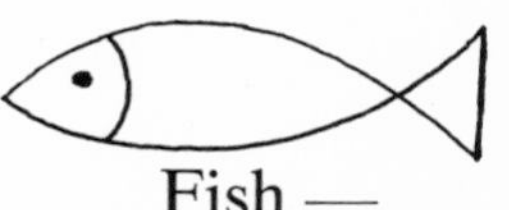

Fish — Symbol for Christ

Sun Symbols

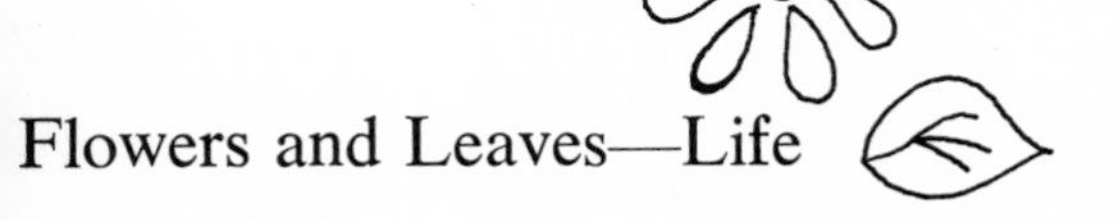

Flowers and Leaves—Life

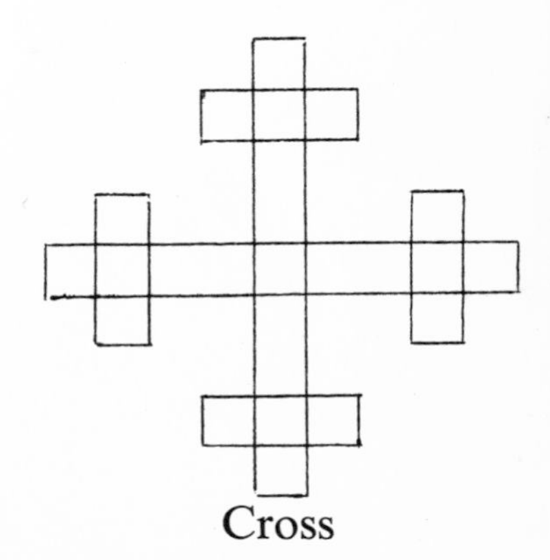

Cross

Figure 2

countries are taught this egg art when they are very young, but it takes many years to become expert.

4. After the design is painted and thoroughly dry, spray the egg with gloss fixative.

There are several books showing Czechoslovakian and Ukrainian egg designs. Some are listed at the back of this book. Others may be available at your local library.

Polish Paper-cut Eggs

You Will Need:

plain egg painted white (jumbo chicken or duck egg if possible)
fixative
stiff colored paper (stationery, origami or construction)
tissue paper in assorted colors (small pieces or scraps)
white glue and brush
scissors
button or jar lid about 1 inch diameter
sewing needle and strong thread
paper punch

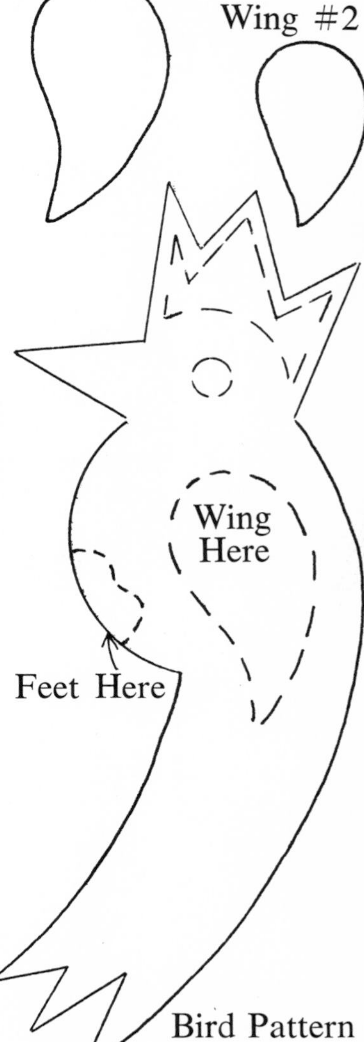

How to Make It:

1. Trace patterns for bird, both wing sections, and feet, then transfer them to colored papers. Cut out 2 birds (from red paper if possible), 4 feet from a different-colored paper, 2 crowns and 4 large wings from another color, and 4 small wings from still another color. (The colors most used for Polish paper-cut eggs are red, white, bright blue, bright yellow, and dark green.)

2. To assemble 1 bird, glue 1 foot to one side of a bird body where indicated on the pattern, then glue another foot to the

Figure 1

other side of the body. *Do not* glue feet together. Glue one small wing on top of a large wing. Glue wing to body where indicated on the pattern. Make another wing and glue it on the other side of the body. Next, paste a crown on each side of the head. Punch 2 dots from black paper with a paper punch. Glue one on each side of the head for eyes. Make another bird in the same way. When birds are thoroughly dry, bend out feet in opposite directions.

3. Spray white egg with fixative and let dry, then attach a bird to each side. Put glue on the bottom of the feet and glue a bird to one side of the egg (Fig. 1). The feet should be placed at about the middle of the egg. Glue the other bird on the other side of the egg, exactly opposite the first so that the two birds face each other (Fig. 2).

4. Polish people fold paper in half and,

Figure 2

without a pattern, cut out beautiful and intricate shapes of flowers, birds, leaves, and scrolls. When the paper is opened flat, the design is a perfectly symmetrical shape. If you wish you may fold colored paper in half and cut your own small designs to decorate your egg. Or trace the flower, leaf, and scroll designs, transfer them to colored paper, and cut out 2 of each piece. Most Polish paper designs are composed of one basic shape with smaller shapes of different colors pasted on top. Glue your cutout paper designs to the front and the back of your egg, centering them between the two birds (Fig. 3). Set egg aside to dry.

Cut-paper Design

Figure 3

5. Next make the hanging thread. Construct 3 paper pompons as follows. Tracing around a jar lid or button, draw 30 circles (10 for each pompon) on tissue paper. Cut out each circle. Thread a needle with a long double strand of strong string and knot one end (Fig. 4).

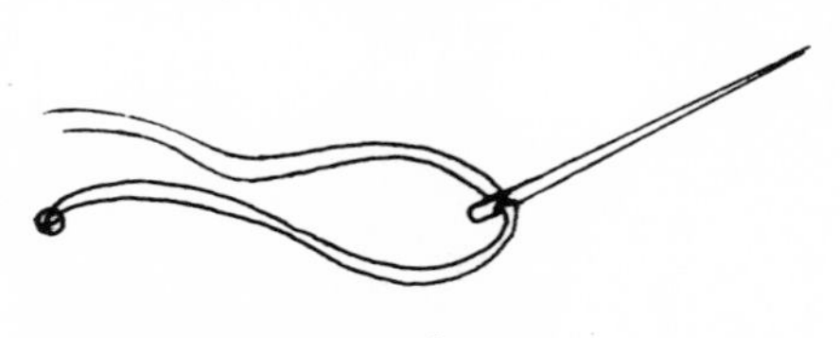

Figure 4

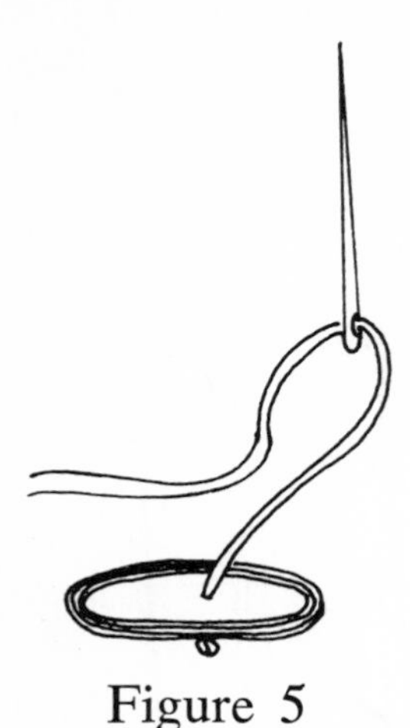

Figure 5

Put 10 circles together in a pile and push the needle through the centers of all the paper circles (Fig. 5). Push all the circles to the end of the thread and tie a knot in the thread just above the pompon. Using scissors, snip into the edges of the pompon circles to fringe them, then shape and separate each layer until you have a pompon shape (Fig. 6).

6. Following method 3 on page 27 (Methods of Hanging Eggs), pull hanging thread through the completed egg. Following instructions in step 5, thread 10 more paper circles to make another pompon on the same thread to top the egg. Knot the thread above the pompon, then knot it again about 1 inch above the pompon and add the last paper circles. Tie another knot in the thread just above this final pompon. Remove needle and, allowing enough thread for a hanging loop, tie ends together.

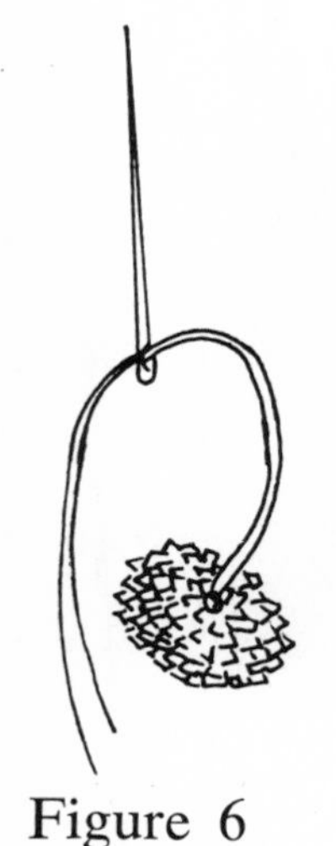

Figure 6

Mexican Cascarones

You Will Need:

plain egg painted black or a very bright color, with a large hole about the size of a quarter in the top (small end)
small piece of tissue paper
stiff colored paper
small package of confetti (can be purchased at party supply counters)
glue, scissors, pencil, narrow braid

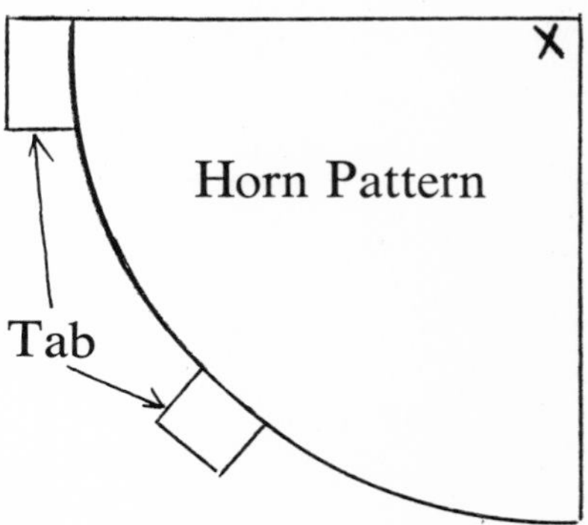

How to Make It:

1. Trace pattern for horn and transfer it to colored paper. Cut out 5 horns. Cut tissue paper into 15 very narrow strips about 2 inches long. You will need 3 strips for each horn. Put a dab of glue on one horn shape where indicated by X on the pattern. Lay one end of 3 tissue-paper strips on top. Do the same thing with the other paper horns. When glue is dry, brush a line of glue along one straight edge of horn shape. Then lap the glued edge over the other straight edge to form a cone (Fig. 1). Be sure the glued ends of the tissue-paper strips are on the inside of the horn and the long ends are sticking out the point. Form the other 4 horns into cones in the same way. Bend tabs of each horn toward the

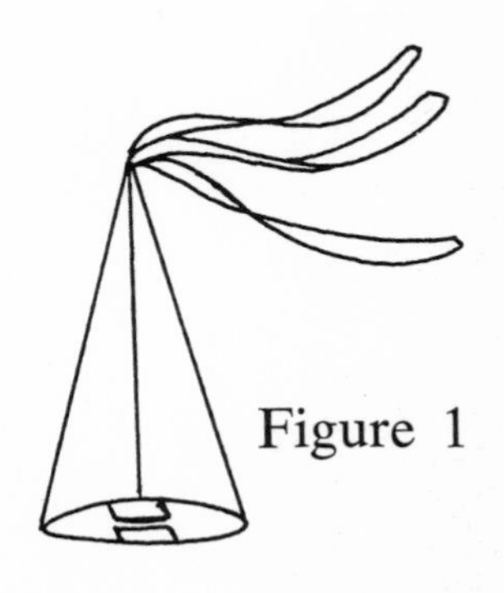
Figure 1

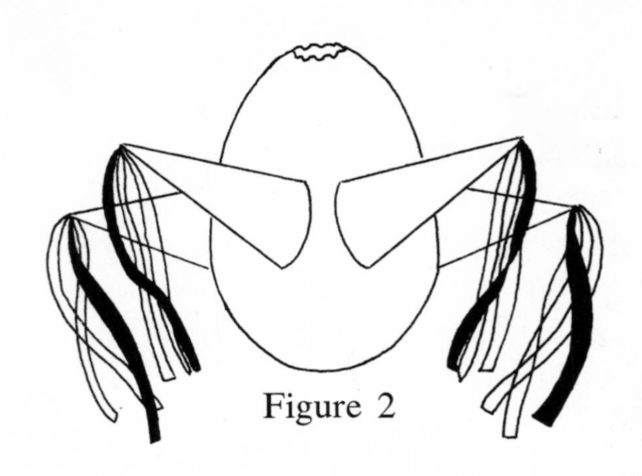
Figure 2

Figure 3

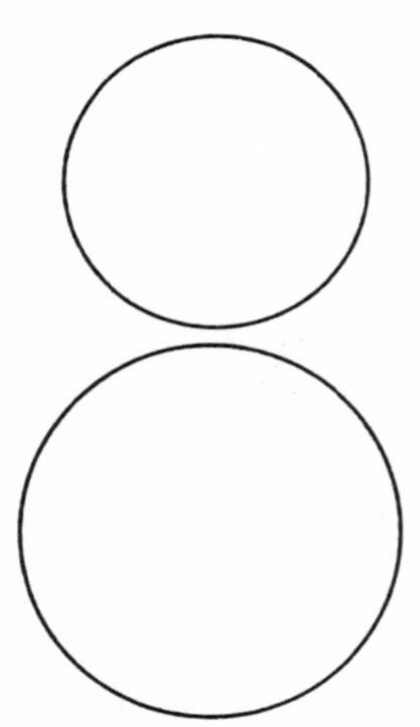
Figure 4

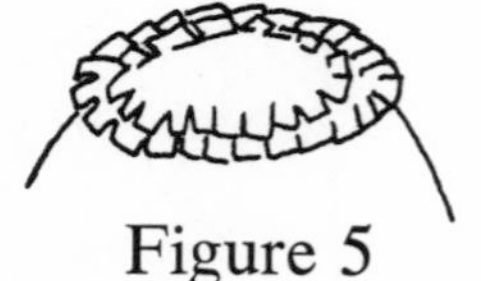
Figure 5

inside of the cone. Put glue on the tabs and glue the 5 horns evenly spaced around the center of the egg (Fig. 2).

3. Using the suggested design in Figure 3 as a guide, cut flowers and leaves from stiff colored paper. Glue leaves and flowers to egg in an allover design.

4. Cut a large and small circle like those in Figure 4 from colored paper. Snipping edges with scissors, fringe both circles. Glue the small circle on top of the large one, then glue the large circle to the bottom of the egg (Fig. 5).

5. Fill the egg with confetti, pouring it into the hole at the top of the egg. Following step 4, cover the hole with a paper circle.

6. To hang the cascarones, cut 3 pieces of braid about 4 inches long. Put glue on one end of each piece and glue the

braid strands evenly spaced around the top of the egg. When glue is dry, knot the free ends of all three strands together (Fig. 6).

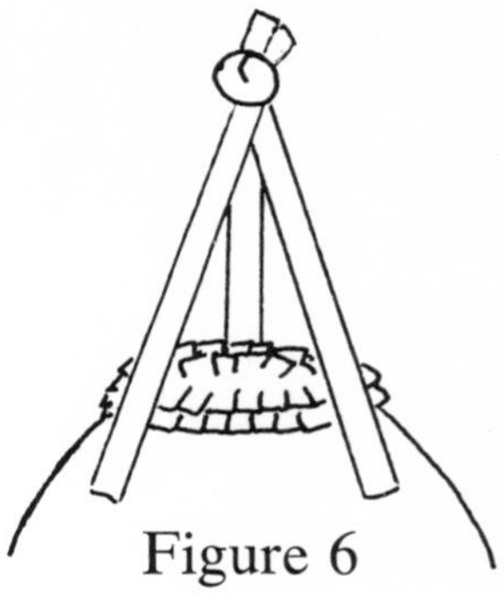

Figure 6

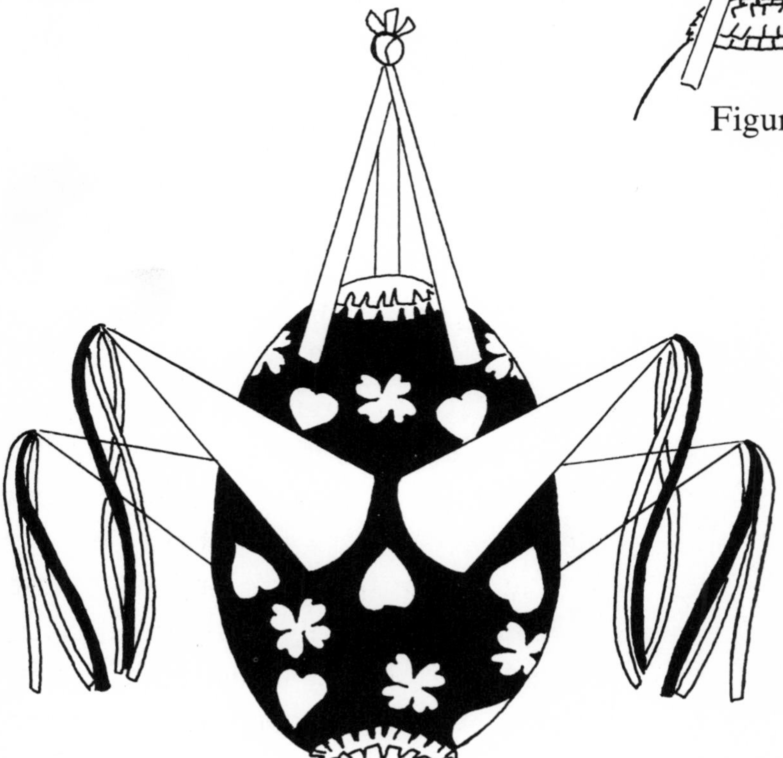

Boutique Eggs

By now you should be quite experienced with egg-crafting and be ready to create an entirely different kind of egg—the dressed-up, fancy egg. The eggs in this chapter will teach you a variety of new techniques. When you master them you'll be on your way to becoming an advanced egger. And no doubt when you complete the last egg in this book, the diorama egg, your creative mind will be working on new ideas and new things to do with eggs. But that's the way it should be. A true egger never wants for ideas because one egg leads to the inspiration for another.

Make-believe Sugar

You Will Need:

plain egg, painted white
small candy flowers and leaves, the kind used for decorating birthday cakes (available at supermarkets)
frosting (see recipe on page 30)
white glue and brush
diamond dust (a crystal glitter resembling sugar)
round toothpicks
narrow ribbon bow (optional)
small shallow box lid

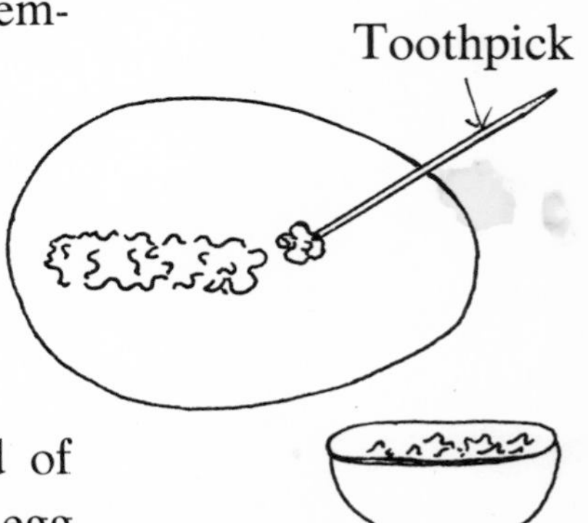

Figure 1

How to Make It:

1. Using a toothpick, apply a band of frosting lengthwise around the white egg (Fig. 1). Set egg aside to dry. (Note: Different brands of paint affect the frosting recipe differently. As frosting dries, it sometimes shrinks too fast and large cracks appear. If cracks occur, use a paintbrush and paint over the frosting band with a thin layer of more frosting thinned with water to a brushing consistency. This coat of thinned frosting will fill the cracks. If only fine-line cracks occur, they can be filled in with a coat of white paint.)
2. When frosting band is dry, arrange

Press Flower Into Frosting

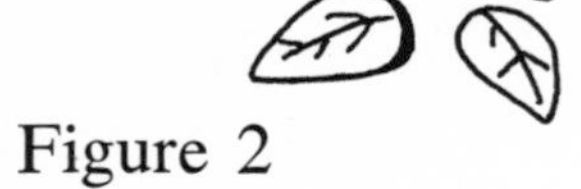

Figure 2

flowers and leaves on top of egg. First apply a small glob of frosting where you plan to put the flowers, then immediately brush backs of flowers with glue and press them into the frosting (Fig. 2). Let frosting dry.

3. Now apply the "sugar" to your egg. Brush a thin layer of glue over a section of the egg surface. Do not put glue on the frosting or flowers. Hold egg over a shallow box lid and sprinkle diamond dust on the wet glue (Fig. 3). The box lid will catch the loose glitter. Continue to brush on glue and sprinkle on diamond dust until the egg surface is covered. Let dry, then gently brush loose glitter off egg, catching it in the box lid. Pour the loose glitter from the lid into a container and save it for another "sugar" egg.

4. Glue a small ribbon bow to the top of the egg with the flowers if desired.

For your next "sugar" egg, use a pastel pink or green egg for a deliciously different effect.

Figure 3

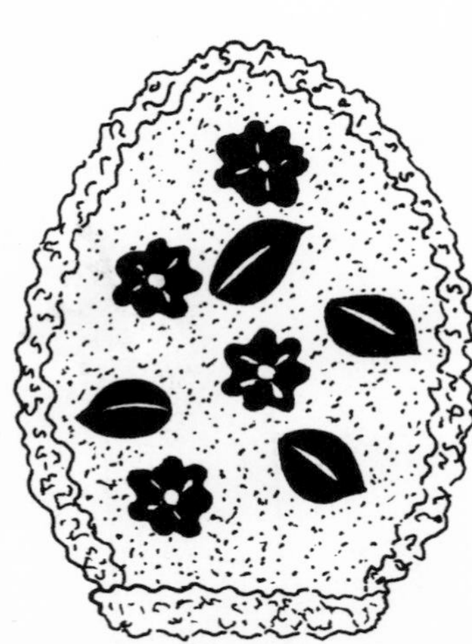

Mosaic Flower

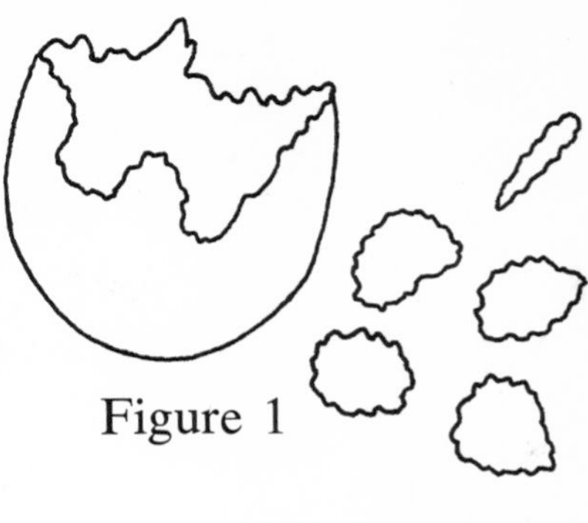
Figure 1

You Will Need:
plain egg painted any pastel or light color
dyed broken shells (see page 25)
green and yellow paints
fine-point paintbrush or fine-line felt markers
glue and small brush
tweezers (optional)
spray fixative

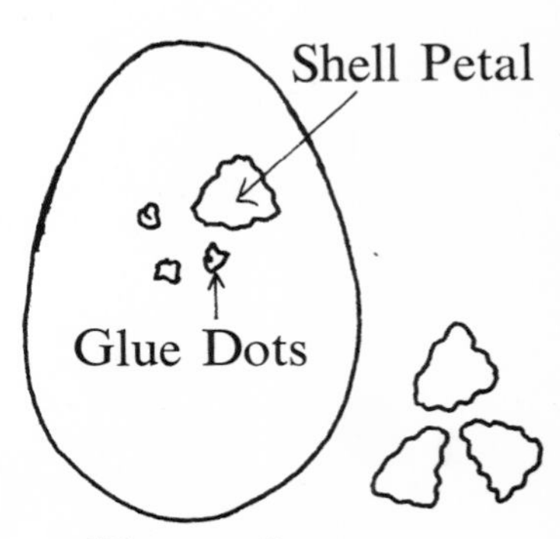

Figure 2

How to Make It:

1. Mosaic flowers are made from small pieces of egg shell broken from larger dyed shell fragments. Break off an assortment of small shell shapes (Fig. 1). Select 4 or 5 pieces which look like petals and which are similar in size and shape. Apply 4 or 5 dots of glue in a circle on the plain egg surface and press a shell petal on each dot (Fig. 2). (You can use tweezers to hold and place the small shell pieces if desired.)

Figure 3

2. When glue has dried, paint on stems and leaves with green paint, and flower centers using yellow (Fig. 3). If desired, you may add some white or light-colored shading to each petal (Fig. 4). When paint is dry, spray egg with fixative.

Figure 4

3. You can decorate plain eggs with all-over mosaic flower designs or with flower sprays. Make some flowers with large wide petals, others with small narrow petals. Leaves, too, can be made from pieces of shell.

Beaded Eggs

You Will Need:

plain egg painted with bright-colored nail polish
an assortment of sequins, seed and bugle beads, and small pearls
round toothpicks
glue
small piece of cardboard
pencil
kneaded eraser

How to Make It:

1. Study the illustrations of the finished eggs. Select one of the designs shown or create one of your own. There are many ways beads can be used to create designs on eggs. Lightly sketch the outline of the design you have chosen on the egg with pencil, or just make pencil dots wherever you plan to put a bead.

2. Tear a tiny piece off the kneaded eraser and knead it into a ball. Push the ball onto the end of a toothpick (Fig. 1). This tool you have just created will make the job of picking up and placing the tiny beads much easier. Tiny beads will stick to the eraser, enabling you to place them on the egg shell exactly where you want them. Occasionally remove the

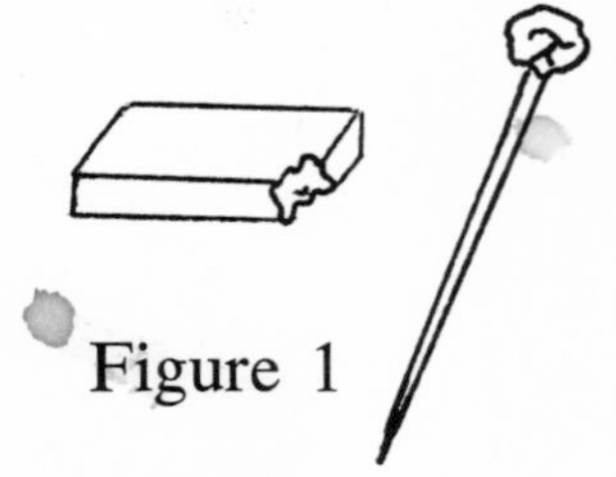

Figure 1

eraser ball and knead it again to keep it soft.

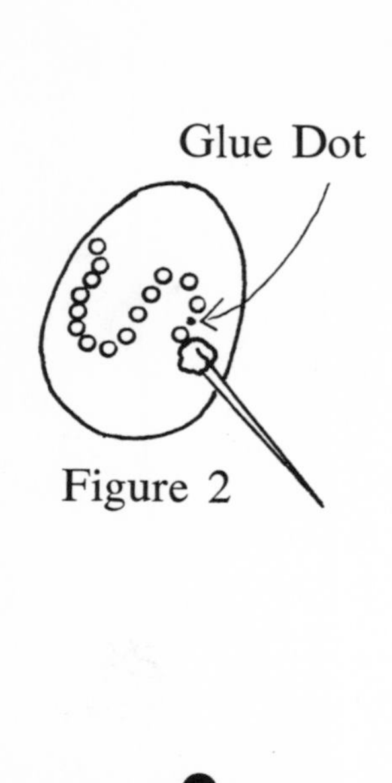

Figure 2

3. Put a small glob of glue on the piece of cardboard. Dip the end of another toothpick in the glue and apply a dot of glue on the shell where a bead is to be placed. Using your tool, pick up a bead and press it into the glue dot. Repeat this step until your drawn outline is completely covered with beads (Fig. 2).

Now you can experiment with other bead designs. Instead of just following outlines, you may wish to fill in small areas like leaves and flower petals solidly with beads. You might also try combining beads with metallic braids and rickrack to obtain another type of decorated egg.

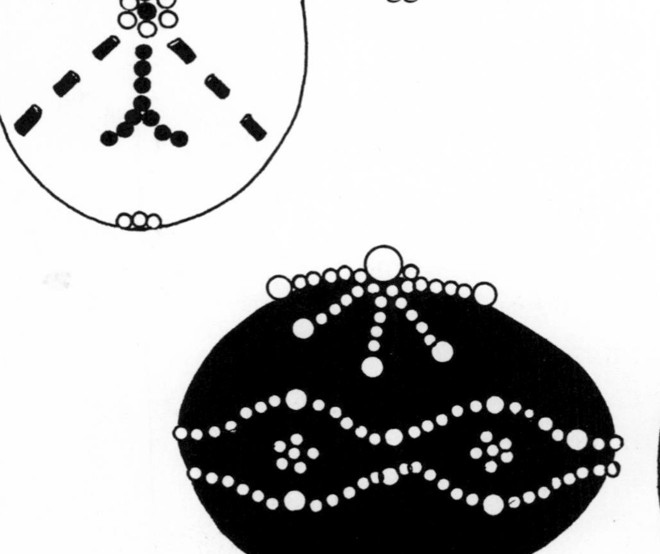

Stained-glass Egg

You Will Need:
plain egg painted white
gloss fixative
tissue paper in assorted colors
polymer medium and paintbrush
scissors
very narrow black braid or cord
glue and a small brush

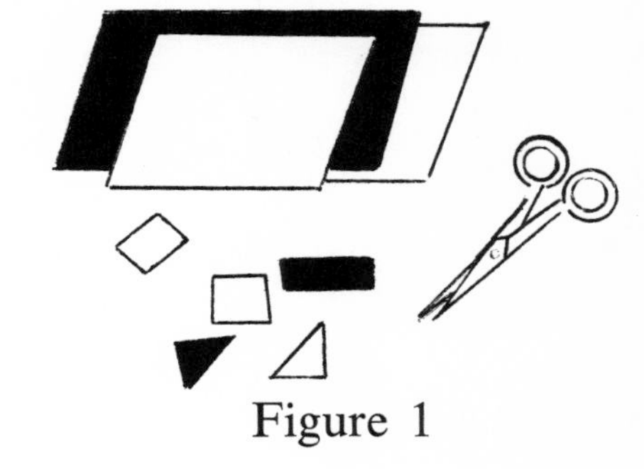
Figure 1

How to Make It:
1. Spray or brush white painted egg with gloss fixative. Let dry.
2. Cut tissue paper into small squares, rectangles, triangles, and strips about 1 × 1 inch in size (Fig. 1). Do not use too many different colors on one egg. Use color combinations that look good together such as brown, yellow, orange, and green; or red, blue, green, and yellow.
3. Brush a small area of the egg with polymer medium. Immediately cover this area with a tissue-paper shape (Fig. 2). The paper will wrinkle slightly, but try to apply it as smoothly as possible. Brush polymer medium on the egg right next to the first paper shape. Lay another paper piece on top, slightly overlapping the first paper shape (Fig. 3). Repeat this

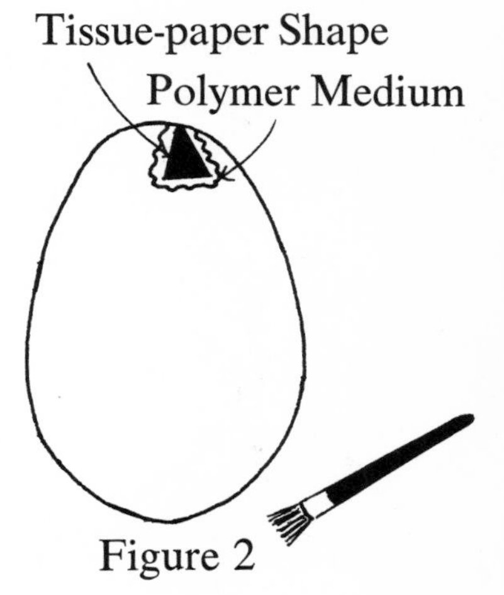

Figure 2

Figure 3

Figure 4

Figure 5

step until the egg is completely covered with a layer of tissue-paper shapes (Fig. 4). Now brush the complete egg with a coat of polymer medium.

4. When egg is thoroughly dry, glue narrow braid in a continuous abstract line around the egg to simulate black leading. Starting at the top of the egg, use a small brush to apply a short narrow glue line on the egg surface. Press braid neatly on the glue line. Apply more glue, then more braid (Fig. 5). Continue until braid is applied around egg and you are back where you began at the top of the egg.

5. Make a small bow using braid. Glue bow to top of egg where the braid ends meet.

Next time you create a stained-glass egg, try beginning with a plain egg painted silver.

Pewter

Figure 1

You Will Need:
plain egg, unpainted
white lace-paper doily
glue and brush
scissors
black paint and brush
fixative
silver metallic rub-on paste (such as Rub 'n Buff)

How to Make It:
1. Cut out designs from the paper doily (Fig. 1). These designs can be scrolls, circles, leaves, scallops, or flowers, depending on the pattern of your particular doily. Using your small design pieces, decide how to arrange them on the egg shell in an allover pleasing pattern. Brush a thin layer of glue on the back of each piece and stick all of them in place on the egg (Fig. 2). Make certain that all parts of each piece are glued flat against the egg shell. Let glue dry.
2. Paint complete egg black, taking care to get paint in all depressions and openings of design so that no white of egg or doily shows. It may be best to paint egg with 2 coats of paint, but let the first coat dry before applying the second. Put egg

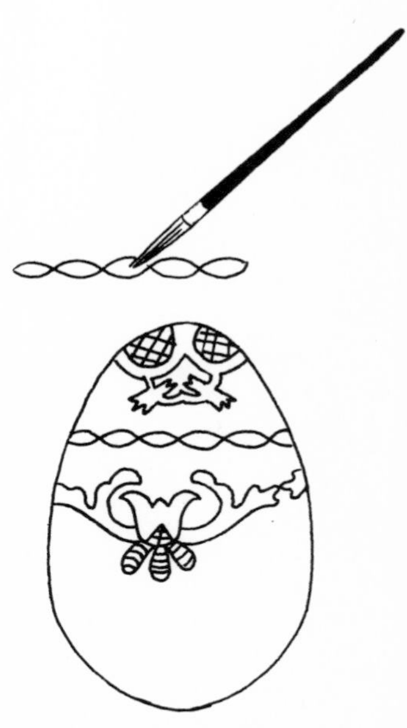
Figure 2

aside to dry for several hours. Then spray lightly with fixative.

3. To give your embossed egg a pewter-like finish, squeeze a small amount of silver metallic paste on your finger and gently rub over all parts of the raised design, allowing the black paint to show in the recesses. Polish egg gently with a soft cloth.

Ribbons and Lace

You Will Need:

plain egg painted very pale pink, yellow, blue, or green (or use a white or pearl nail polish)
narrow ribbon, lace, gold or silver metallic braid
sewing needle and threads (to match lace and ribbon)
glue and small brush
scissors
tiny by-the-yard pearls (these pearls come in a long string and can be cut to any length desired)

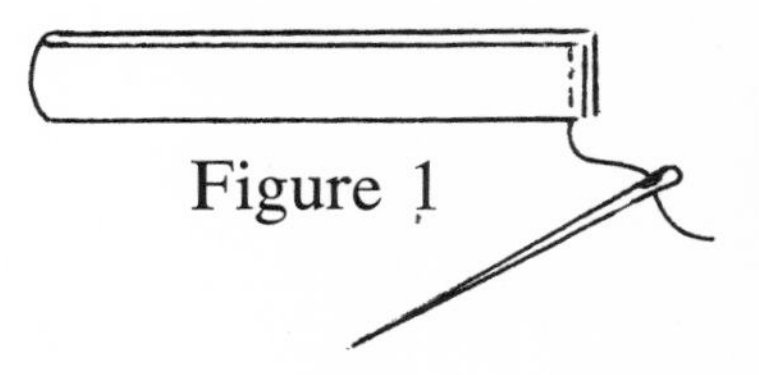
Figure 1

How to Make It:

1. To make flowers, cut a 2- to 3-inch length of narrow satin ribbon. (Length of ribbon will depend on the size flower you wish to make.) With matching thread, sew the two short ends together so that ribbon will form a ring (Fig. 1). Next, sew a row of running stitches along one straight edge of the ribbon ring (Fig. 2). Pull up stitches to gather ribbon tightly. Ribbon will form a circle-like flower (Fig. 3). Fasten thread securely.

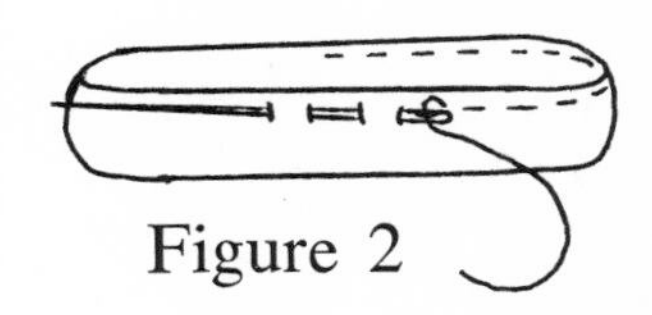
Figure 2

2. Study the illustrations of the completed eggs, and, using them for inspiration, create your own ribbon-and-lace

Figure 3

egg. Use a fine brush to apply thin lines of glue to the egg shell when attaching ribbons, lace, braids, or pearl trimming. Before applying lace to the egg, gather the straight edge slightly. Use only dots of glue for sticking on ribbon flowers, then glue a small pearl in the center of each flower. You do not have to put braids, ribbons, lace, bows, flowers, and pearls all on one egg. Lovely eggs can be created using just ribbons, lace, and a few flowers. And equally pretty eggs can be made by using metallic braids, pearls, and pastel-colored lace.

Ribbon-and-lace eggs are meant to look fragile and delicate, so take extra time to be extra neat when creating them.

Glittering Jewels

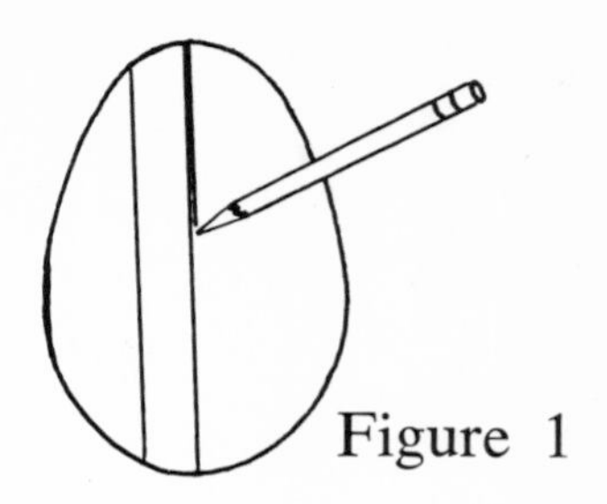
Figure 1

You Will Need:
large plain egg, unpainted
very narrow metallic braid (adhesive-backed braid is very easy to use)
glitter in gold and another color such as red or green
about 8 flat-back paste-on, diamond-shaped jewels
glue and paintbrush
2 small shallow bowls
pencil
wide rubber band
scissors

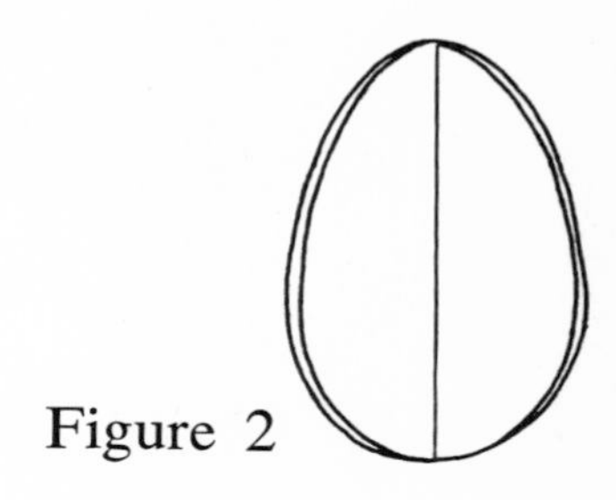
Figure 2

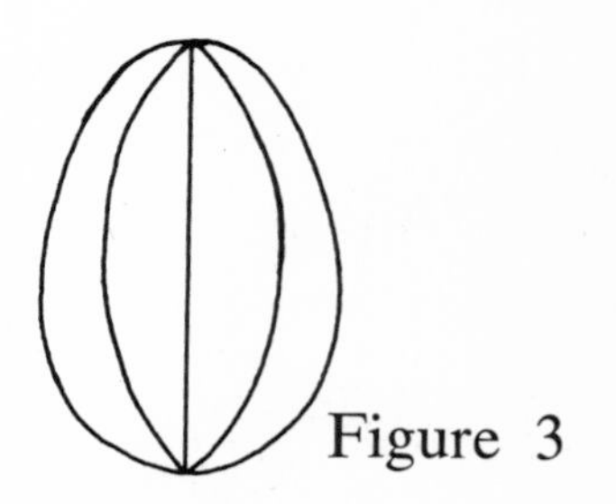
Figure 3

How to Make It:
1. Using the pencil and rubber band, divide egg in half lengthwise (Fig. 1), then in quarters (Fig. 2), then into eighths (Fig. 3). The rubber band is used as a guide to help you draw straight lines on the egg. Place the rubber band around the middle of the egg and draw a band about ¾ inch wide (Fig. 4).

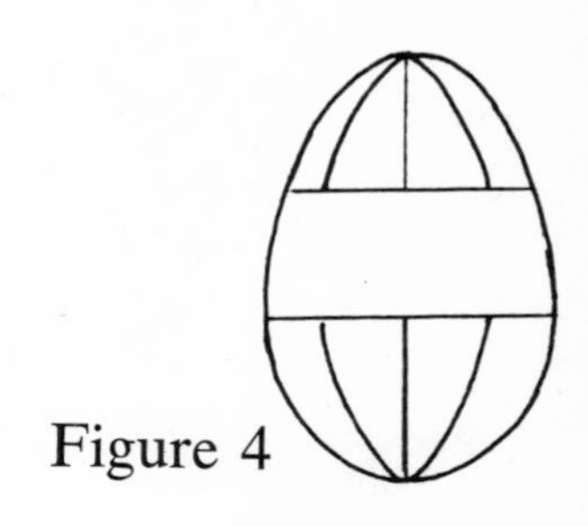
Figure 4

2. With brush, paint a narrow line of glue around the egg on one of the penciled band lines. Press narrow braid on the glue line (Fig. 5). Do the same thing on the other penciled band line, then on all lines above and below the band

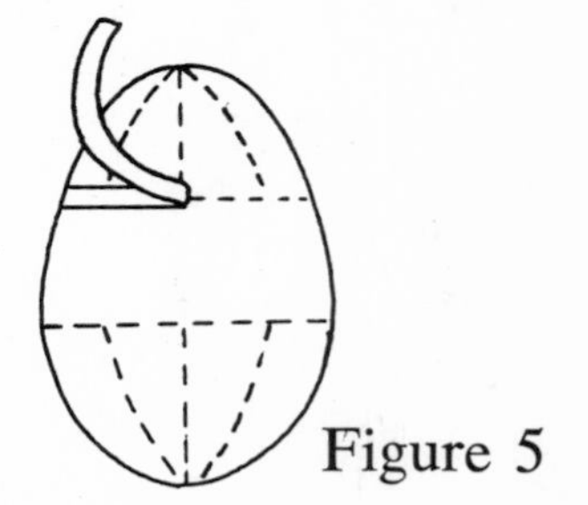
Figure 5

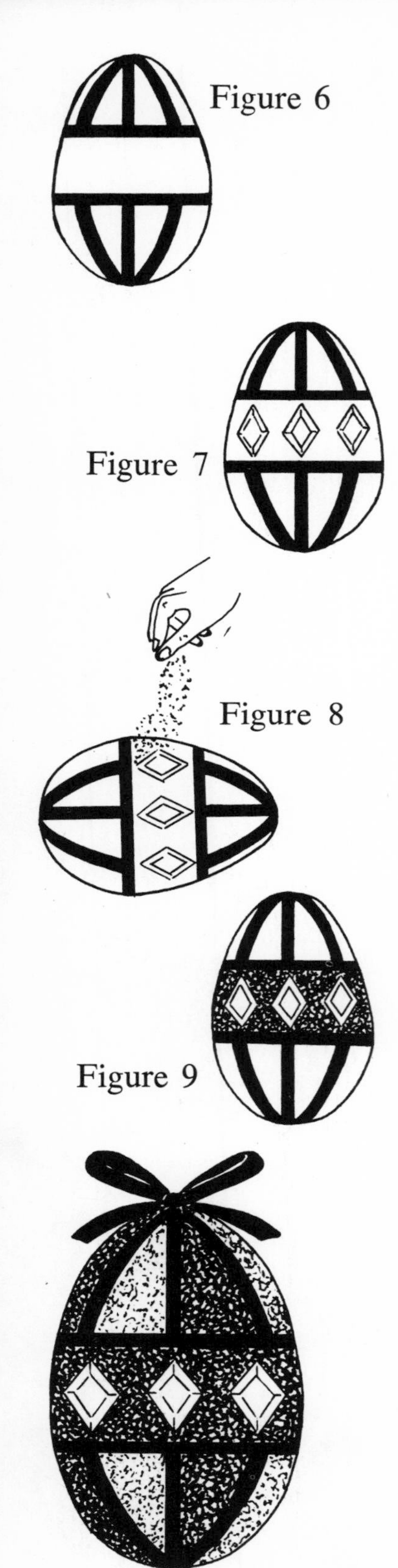

(Fig. 6). If you are using adhesive-backed braid, follow Step 2 but omit applying glue.

3. Glue flat-backed jewels evenly spaced around egg within the center band (Fig. 7). Let glue dry.

4. Pour gold glitter in one of the small bowls. Pour the other color glitter in the other bowl. With brush, and working on just a small section at a time, apply glue to the egg shell in the center band area. Be careful not to get glue on the braid or jewels. Holding egg over the bowl, sprinkle gold glitter on the wet glue with your fingers (Fig. 8). Continue to apply glue and glitter until the entire shell in the band area is covered. Now, with a pencil, mark a G on alternate eighth sections around the egg, above and below the band (Fig. 9). Apply gold glitter to all the areas marked with a G. Let glue dry thoroughly, then gently brush loose glitter off egg and into the proper bowl.

5. On all the remaining eighth sections, apply green or another color glitter. When egg is complete, return glitter to its original container and save for another egg.

6. Make a small bow of gold braid and glue it to the top of the finished egg.

Découpage

You Will Need:

plain egg, painted a light color
small picture from greeting card, gift wrapping paper, or stationery
polymer medium and brush
manicure scissors with curved blades
waxed paper
spray fixative
glue and brush
damp sponge
découpage spray

How to Make It:

1. To learn the techniques of découpage, make your first egg a simple one using a small single picture. Brush the surface of your selected picture with a coat of polymer medium (Fig. 1) or spray the picture with fixative. This will seal the colored inks and strengthen the paper for cutting. While your picture is drying, spray the egg with fixative to seal the painted surface.

Figure 1

2. Using curved manicure scissors, cut out your print. Remove all parts of the background within the picture first, then cut away all excess paper around the outside of the picture. When using manicure scissors, be sure the blades curve away

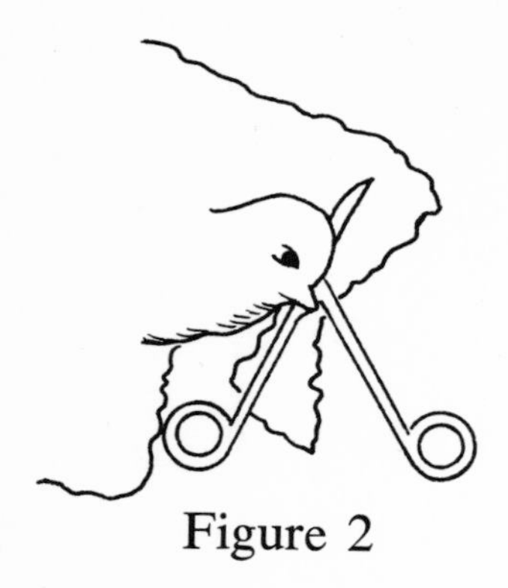
Figure 2

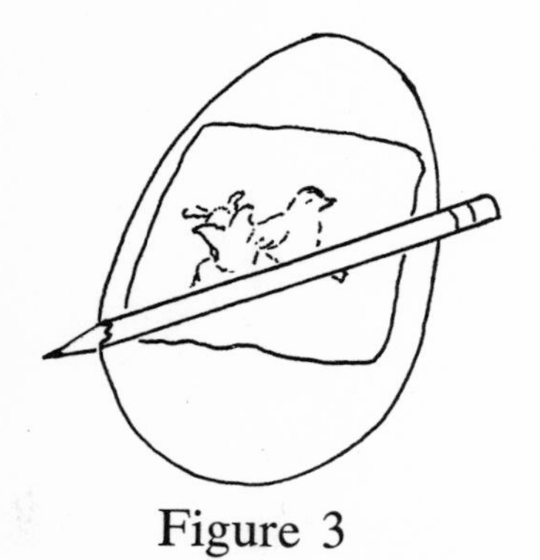
Figure 3

from the picture (Fig. 2). This will give the cutout print a beveled edge which will fit tight against the egg shell when glued in place.

3. Lay your cutout face-down on a small piece of waxed paper and brush a thin layer of glue over the back. Gently pick up the picture and carefully stick it to the egg. With your fingers, press it tightly against the egg surface. Lay another small piece of waxed paper over the picture and, working from the center to the outside edge, roll a pencil over the print, pressing gently to make sure all parts are pressed down tight and to force out excess glue (Fig. 3). Remove waxed paper and wipe away all excess glue with a damp sponge. Set egg aside until thoroughly dry, about 24 hours. (If you rush this step and the print is not dry, air bubbles may later appear in the print and ruin the finished egg.) Spray the complete egg with fixative and let dry.

4. This step of applying the découpage finish means burying the picture under a coating of varnish or glaze so that you can no longer feel the edge of the print with your fingers and the picture appears to be under glass. For a quicky project, apply 3 to 5 coats of polymer medium to the complete egg. Allow 30 minutes for

each coat to dry before applying the next. This polymer medium method, although quick and easy, will not give your egg a smooth crystal-clear coating, but instead a clear, somewhat textured finish will result. For a more professional method of découpage use a clear plastic spray, following the directions on the can for application and drying time between coats. Generally 3 to 5 light coats should be sufficient to bury the picture and give your egg a crystal-clear glaze.

5. Now découpage another egg, but this time instead of using just one picture apply several cutouts all over the egg surface, or use several cutouts to create a scene.

Miniature Vase

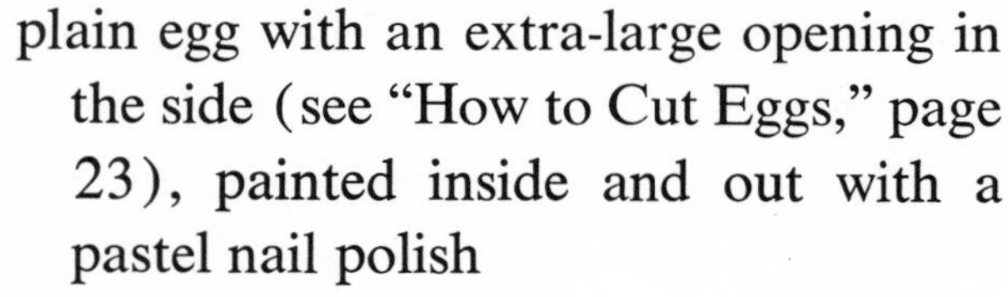

You Will Need:

plain egg with an extra-large opening in the side (see "How to Cut Eggs," page 23), painted inside and out with a pastel nail polish

assortment of beads

gold-colored curtain ring, about 1 inch in diameter

small styrofoam ball (green if desired)

bunch of tiny artificial or dried flowers

small piece of absorbent cotton

glue, toothpicks, scissors

Curtain Ring

Figure 1

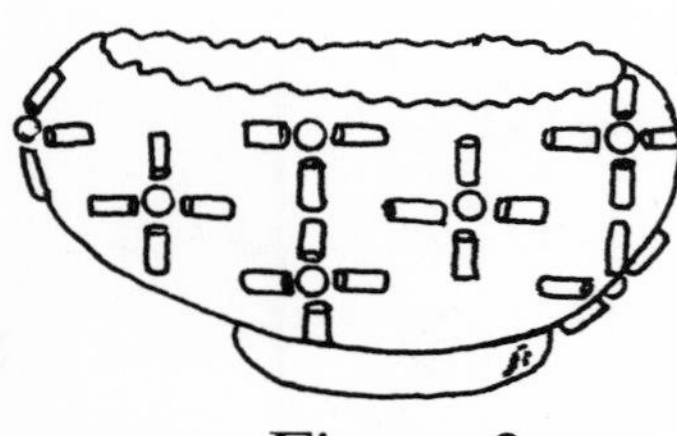

Figure 2

How to Make It:

1. Glue curtain ring to the bottom of the egg (Fig. 1). Let glue dry.

2. Decorate egg with an all-over bead design like the one shown in Figure 2, or in any manner you wish. (See Beaded Eggs, page 105, for method of applying beads.) Set egg aside to dry.

Figure 3

3. Flatten one side of the small styrofoam ball by pressing it against a flat surface (Fig. 3). Now arrange a bouquet of flowers. If the flowers you are using are taped together, remove the tape so that you will have single flowers to work with. Insert stems in the round side of the styrofoam ball (Fig. 4). Cut some of

Figure 4

the stems shorter than others so that flowers will not be all the same height.

4. When you have arranged all the flowers in the ball, brush a layer of glue over the flat bottom of the ball. Immediately stick a thin layer of absorbent cotton on the glue. Next, put a puddle of glue inside the bottom of the egg-shell vase and insert your bouquet. The cotton will help the styrofoam ball stick quickly to the bottom of the shell.

Diorama

You Will Need:

diorama egg (see "How to Cut Eggs," page 23) painted light blue inside and any desired color outside
½ of a small green styrofoam ball
picture of an animal or bird cut from a greeting card (about 1 inch tall or a size to fit inside your egg)
polymer medium and paintbrush
toothpick
tiny artificial flowers
narrow metallic braids (use a single looped edge braid if possible)
tiny prestrung pearls and several large beads or pearls
plastic curtain ring, about 1 inch in diameter
manicure scissors and regular scissors
fixative
glue and brush
small piece of absorbent cotton

How to Make It:

1. There are many varieties of diorama eggs. Some are elaborately decorated on the outside with beads and lace and other trimmings. Some have beautiful little scenes inside, using tiny glass, ceramic, or plastic figures, plus artificial trees and

flowers. Each egger designs and constructs a diorama egg differently. You too can create elaborate diorama eggs after you make a few simple ones. So, begin with this easy scene for a simple but pretty egg. Brush a coat of polymer medium over the animal picture you have selected. Let dry, then brush on another coat. Paint the back of the picture too. This acrylic coating will strengthen the paper and give it a glossy shine.

2. Using manicure scissors, cut out your animal or bird. With a brush, apply a line of glue in the back of the cutout lengthwise from the top to the bottom, then stick the end of the toothpick on the glue line (Fig. 1). (Don't allow the toothpick to show above the top of your animal.) The toothpick will become the stand for your cutout. Put some glue on the bottom end of the toothpick and push it into the green styrofoam half ball (Fig. 2). Brush glue over the flat bottom of the ball and press a thin layer of absorbent cotton on the glue (Fig. 3). The cotton will help your scene grab hold quickly when you put it inside the egg.

3. Spray the diorama egg shell inside and out with fixative and let dry. Carefully put a puddle of glue inside the bottom of the egg at the broad end. Gently set the

Figure 1

Figure 2

Figure 3

Figure 4

Figure 5

styrofoam half ball on the glue puddle (Fig. 4). Set egg aside until glue dries and styrofoam ball is securely set in place.

4. Now trim the outside shell. With a brush, apply a thin line of glue around the cut edge of the shell opening. (Do only a short length at a time; otherwise glue will dry before you have a chance to put on the trim.) Beginning at the top of the opening, press narrow braid in place on the glue line (Fig. 5). Next, brush a line of glue around the egg right next to the row of braid and glue a row of tiny-pearl trimming in place (Fig. 6). Make a bow of braid and glue it at the top of the egg opening over the spot where the two ends of the braid row meet (Fig. 7).

5. To make a stand for your egg, apply glue to the curtain ring and set egg on the ring. Now trim the top of the egg with

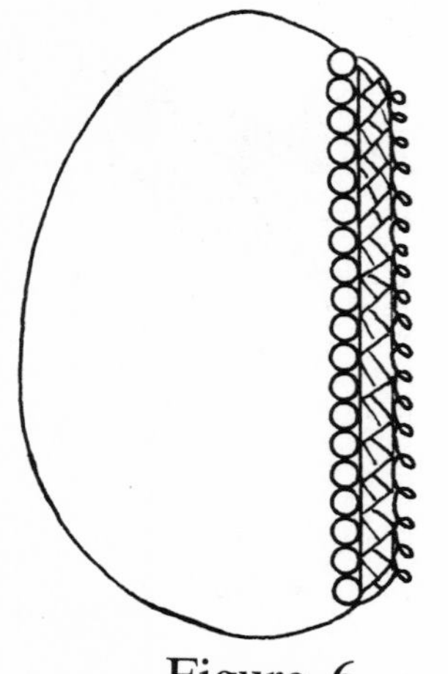

Figure 6

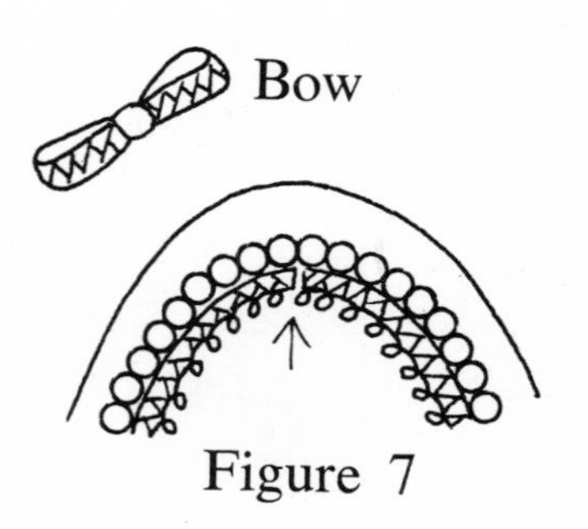

Figure 7

several fancy beads or pearls glued one on top of the other (Fig. 8).

6. Finally, cut almost all the stems off several tiny artificial flowers. Put glue on the backs of the flowers and stick them to the styrofoam ball inside the egg. Arrange the flowers attractively around your animal figure.

Now you have a general idea of how a diorama egg is constructed. The next egg you make could be completely covered on the outside with rows of beads and metallic braid. And the inside scene could be a wintry one, using a tiny skiing figure and diamond dust for snow.

Figure 8

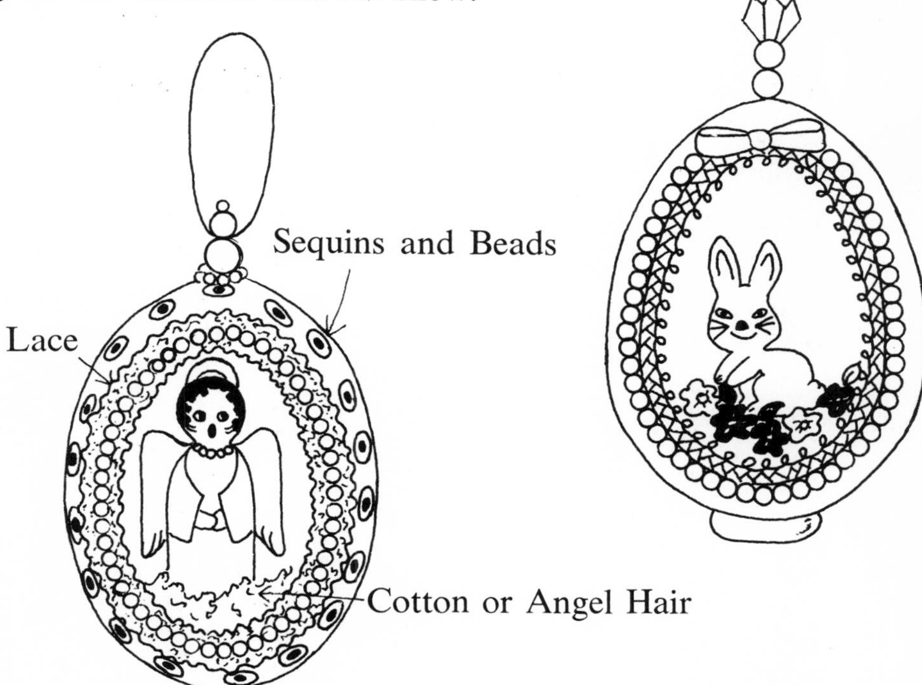

Diorama Egg With Tiny Wooden Angel Inside

Books to Read

About Eggs

THE EGG TREE, by Katherine Milhous. New York: Charles Scribner's Sons, 1950.

EASTERTIDE IN PENNSYLVANIA: A FOLK CULTURAL STUDY, by Alfred L. Shoemaker. Kutztown, Pa.: Pennsylvania Folklife Society, 1960.

PETER CARL FABERGÉ: GOLDSMITH AND JEWELER TO THE RUSSIAN IMPERIAL COURT, by Henry Charles Bainbridge. London: Spring Books, 1942.

THE ART OF CARL FABERGÉ, by A. Kenneth Snowman. London: Faber & Faber, Ltd., 1962.

AN EGG AT EASTER: A FOLKLORE STUDY, by Venetia Newell. Bloomington, Ind.: Indiana University Press, 1971.

About Egg Craft

EGG DECORATING, by Nancy Lang. New York: Bruce Publishing Co., 1971.

Pamphlets

BEJEWELED EGGS
Hazel Pearson Handicrafts
4128 Temple City Blvd.
Rosemead, Calif. 91770

UKRAINIAN EASTER EGGS
by Yaroslava Surmach
Surma
11 East 7th Street
New York, N. Y. 10003

PYSANKY INSTRUCTIONS FOR DECORATED EGGS
48 East 7th Street
New York, N. Y. 10003

EGGSTRA by Kit
Kit Stansbury
411 Warren Street
Phillipsburg, N. J. 08865

BEADED EGGS by J. Tickey
5532 N. Persimmon Ave.
Temple City, Calif. 91780

EGGSHELLS TO OBJECTS D'ART
Ima Ova
Box 605
Holland, Mich. 49423

BOUTIQUING EGGS
Graff Publications, Inc.
910 North Marshfield Ave.
Chicago, Ill. 60622

Sources for Supplies

Egg Shells

Julia Hernberg
1702 Corwallis Parkway
Cape Coral, Florida 33904
Several varieties of whole and cut shells. Price list is available.

Anna Hoffman
Hoffman Goose Hatchery
Gratz, Pa. 17030
Goose shells.

Rider Animal Co.
R. R. 2, Box 270
Brooksville, Florida 33512
Variety of shells.

Trimmings (Ribbons, lace, braids, sequins, pearls, and beads)

Home-Sew, Inc.
Bethlehem, Pa. 18018 — Catalog available.

Hazel Pearson Handicrafts
4128 Temple City Blvd.
Rosemead, Calif. 91770 — Catalog available.

Delco Craft Center Inc.
30081 Stephenson Highway
Madison Heights, Mich. 48071

For All Egg-craft Supplies

Taylor House
Bench & Perry Sts.
Galena, Ill. 61036

Catalog available.

Polymer Medium (Hyplar, Liquitex, Mod-Podge, Art-Podge)

Delco Craft Center, Inc.
30081 Stephenson Highway
Madison Heights, Mich. 48071

Bergen Arts & Crafts
P.O. Box 689
Salem, Mass. 01970 Catalog available.

American Handicrafts (See your phone book for the store nearest you.)

Acrylic Paints in Jars

Delco Craft Center, Inc.
30081 Stephenson Highway
Madison Heights, Mich. 48071

American Handicrafts (See your phone book for the store nearest you.)

Hazel Pearson Handicrafts
4128 Temple City Blvd.
Rosemead, Calif. 91770

Ceramic Stains (See your nearest ceramic dealer or write to any of the following manufactures for the dealer nearest you.)

Ceramichrome Inc. (Bisk-Chrome Stains)
P.O. Box 427
Westminster, California 92683

Fiesta Colors
4209 Spencer Street
Torrance, California 90503

Duncan Ceramic Products, Inc. (Bisq-Stain)
P. O. Box 7827
Fresno, California 93727

Index